P9-ARB-288

DISCARDED

Brooks - Cork Library
Shelton State
Community College

DATE DUE

OPPOSING VIEWPOINTS®

ADDICTION

Louise I. Gerdes, *Book Editor*

Bruce Glassman, *Vice President*
Bonnie Szumski, *Publisher*
Helen Cothran, *Managing Editor*

OPPOSING
VIEWPOINTS®
SERIES

GREENHAVEN
PRESS®

Brooks - Cork Library
Shelton State
Community College

THOMSON
—————*—————
GALE

San Diego • Detroit • New York • San Francisco • Cleveland
New Haven, Conn. • Waterville, Maine • London • Munich

© 2005 by Greenhaven Press. Greenhaven Press is an imprint of Thomson Gale, a part of the Thomson Corporation.

Thomson is a trademark and Gale [and Greenhaven Press] are registered trademarks used herein under license.

For more information, contact
Greenhaven Press
27500 Drake Rd.
Farmington Hills, MI 48331-3535
Or you can visit our Internet site at http://www.gale.com

ALL RIGHTS RESERVED.
No part of this work covered by the copyright hereon may be reproduced or used in any form or by any means—graphic, electronic, or mechanical, including photocopying, recording, taping, Web distribution or information storage retrieval systems—without the written permission of the publisher.

Every effort has been made to trace the owners of copyrighted material.

Cover credit: © Photos.com

LIBRARY OF CONGRESS CATALOGING-IN-PUBLICATION DATA

Addiction : opposing viewpoints / Louise I. Gerdes, book editor.
   p. cm. — (Opposing viewpoints series)
Includes bibliographical references and index.
ISBN 0-7377-2216-9 (lib. : alk. paper) — ISBN 0-7377-2217-7 (pbk. : alk. paper)
   1. Compulsive behavior—United States. 2. Substance abuse—United States.
3. Substance abuse—Government policy—United States. 4. Addicts—United States. I. Gerdes, Louise I., 1953– . II. Opposing viewpoints series (Unnumbered)
HV4998.A32 2005
362.29—dc22
                                                  2003067520

Printed in the United States of America

"Congress shall make no law...abridging the freedom of speech, or of the press."

First Amendment to the U.S. Constitution

The basic foundation of our democracy is the First Amendment guarantee of freedom of expression. The Opposing Viewpoints Series is dedicated to the concept of this basic freedom and the idea that it is more important to practice it than to enshrine it.

Contents

Why Consider Opposing Viewpoints?

"The only way in which a human being can make some approach to knowing the whole of a subject is by hearing what can be said about it by persons of every variety of opinion and studying all modes in which it can be looked at by every character of mind. No wise man ever acquired his wisdom in any mode but this."

John Stuart Mill

In our media-intensive culture it is not difficult to find differing opinions. Thousands of newspapers and magazines and dozens of radio and television talk shows resound with differing points of view. The difficulty lies in deciding which opinion to agree with and which "experts" seem the most credible. The more inundated we become with differing opinions and claims, the more essential it is to hone critical reading and thinking skills to evaluate these ideas. Opposing Viewpoints books address this problem directly by presenting stimulating debates that can be used to enhance and teach these skills. The varied opinions contained in each book examine many different aspects of a single issue. While examining these conveniently edited opposing views, readers can develop critical thinking skills such as the ability to compare and contrast authors' credibility, facts, argumentation styles, use of persuasive techniques, and other stylistic tools. In short, the Opposing Viewpoints Series is an ideal way to attain the higher-level thinking and reading skills so essential in a culture of diverse and contradictory opinions.

In addition to providing a tool for critical thinking, Opposing Viewpoints books challenge readers to question their own strongly held opinions and assumptions. Most people form their opinions on the basis of upbringing, peer pressure, and personal, cultural, or professional bias. By reading carefully balanced opposing views, readers must directly confront new ideas as well as the opinions of those with whom they disagree. This is not to simplistically argue that everyone who reads opposing views will—or should—change his or her opinion. Instead, the series enhances readers' understanding of their own views by encouraging confrontation with opposing ideas. Careful examination of others' views can lead to the readers' understanding of the logical inconsistencies in their own opinions, perspective on why they hold an opinion, and the consideration of the possibility that their opinion requires further evaluation.

Evaluating Other Opinions

To ensure that this type of examination occurs, Opposing Viewpoints books present all types of opinions. Prominent spokespeople on different sides of each issue as well as well-known professionals from many disciplines challenge the reader. An additional goal of the series is to provide a forum for other, less known, or even unpopular viewpoints. The opinion of an ordinary person who has had to make the decision to cut off life support from a terminally ill relative, for example, may be just as valuable and provide just as much insight as a medical ethicist's professional opinion. The editors have two additional purposes in including these less known views. One, the editors encourage readers to respect others' opinions—even when not enhanced by professional credibility. It is only by reading or listening to and objectively evaluating others' ideas that one can determine whether they are worthy of consideration. Two, the inclusion of such viewpoints encourages the important critical thinking skill of objectively evaluating an author's credentials and bias. This evaluation will illuminate an author's reasons for taking a particular stance on an issue and will aid in readers' evaluation of the author's ideas.

It is our hope that these books will give readers a deeper understanding of the issues debated and an appreciation of the complexity of even seemingly simple issues when good and honest people disagree. This awareness is particularly important in a democratic society such as ours in which people enter into public debate to determine the common good. Those with whom one disagrees should not be regarded as enemies but rather as people whose views deserve careful examination and may shed light on one's own.

Thomas Jefferson once said that "difference of opinion leads to inquiry, and inquiry to truth." Jefferson, a broadly educated man, argued that "if a nation expects to be ignorant and free . . . it expects what never was and never will be." As individuals and as a nation, it is imperative that we consider the opinions of others and examine them with skill and discernment. The Opposing Viewpoints Series is intended to help readers achieve this goal.

David L. Bender and Bruno Leone,
Founders

Greenhaven Press anthologies primarily consist of previously published material taken from a variety of sources, including periodicals, books, scholarly journals, newspapers, government documents, and position papers from private and public organizations. These original sources are often edited for length and to ensure their accessibility for a young adult audience. The anthology editors also change the original titles of these works in order to clearly present the main thesis of each viewpoint and to explicitly indicate the opinion presented in the viewpoint. These alterations are made in consideration of both the reading and comprehension levels of a young adult audience. Every effort is made to ensure that Greenhaven Press accurately reflects the original intent of the authors included in this anthology.

Introduction

"Absent a clear definition of addiction, researchers will continue finding it very difficult to determine addiction prevalence rates, etiology, or the necessary and sufficient causes that stimulate recovery."

—*Howard J. Shaffer, director of the Harvard Medical School Division on Addictions*

Stephen started using heroin when he was fourteen. His parents discovered his heroin use when his grades began to drop, and they sent Stephen to a rehabilitation center. After treatment, Stephen began to use again and became involved in repeated confrontations with the law. At sixteen, Stephen's parents asked him to leave home. Unable to keep a job, Stephen turned to prostitution to obtain money to buy heroin. Despite his estrangement from family and friends, and in spite of the risk of contracting AIDS from needle sharing and prostitution, Stephen continues to use.

Maryann had been married for fifteen years when she began regularly conversing on Internet chat rooms. Soon she was going to bed later and later in order to spend more time chatting, flirting, and occasionally masturbating with an on-line partner. She felt guilty when she crawled into bed next to her sleeping husband. Each morning she vowed, "Never again." However, the next day she would find herself counting the hours until she could log on again. Although her work and her relationship with her husband have deteriorated, Maryann continues to chat on the Internet late into the night.

While most would consider Stephen an addict, many would not characterize Maryann's behavior as addictive. Indeed, one of the most significant controversies in the addiction debate is whether or not behaviors such as excessive use of the Internet, compulsive sex, or pathological gambling should be considered addictions. Some analysts question whether compulsive behaviors should be lumped together with addictions to substances such as alcohol and heroin. According to Donna Markus, clinical director of AddictionSolutions.com, referring to behaviors as addictive is becoming more common, but professionals have varied views on what should be considered addiction. "Today, it's fairly common to hear the terms 'addict' and 'addiction' applied to a wide variety of behaviors by professionals as well as nonprofessionals," she explains. Nevertheless, she adds, "Although alcohol and other drug addictions have been studied for decades, mental health professionals continue to hold disparate beliefs regarding the etiology and nature of addiction."

In the past, professionals defined addiction as physical dependence on a drug. Craving, increased tolerance, and withdrawal were considered clinical evidence of this dependence. Craving involves an intense desire for the drug, tolerance means that the user needs more and more to achieve the high, and withdrawal is the physical and mental suffering that occurs when drug use is discontinued. Professionals who support this definition of addiction believe that only drugs can induce physiological dependence; thus people can only be addicted to drugs, not behaviors.

As researchers continue to examine addiction and addictive substances, this conception has begun to change. For example, *Science* writer Constance Holden maintains, "Even some seemingly classical addictions don't follow [the traditional] pattern. Cocaine, for example, is highly addictive but causes little withdrawal. And a person who gets hooked on morphine while in the hospital may stop taking the drug without developing an obsession with it." Moreover, director of the Harvard Medical School Division of Addictions Howard J. Shaffer argues, some behaviors seem to induce physiological symptoms. "For example," Shaffer claims, "upon stopping, pathological gamblers who do not use alcohol or other psychoactive drugs often show physical symptoms that appear to be very similar to either narcotics, stimulants, or polysubstance withdrawal."

Advances in neurobiology have also changed traditional conceptions of addiction. Scientists discovered that both drugs and behaviors activate a part of the brain known as the reward center. Drug research revealed that drugs mimic or block the brains neurotransmitters in the reward center and take over the brain's dispensing of the reward—the good feeling people get when they eat or have sex. Psychology professor Alice M. Young explains: "Drugs such as alcohol, nicotine, heroin and cocaine may short-circuit the natural reward pathways that have evolved to ensure that we engage in activities critical to our survival." Thus, in order to get the "reward," the good feeling people often attribute to being high, people must continue to use the drug.

More recently, researchers have found that a habit such as gambling, overeating, excessive sex, or use of the Internet can also hijack the brain's circuitry. According to Stanford University psychologist Brian Knutson, "It stands to reason if you can derange [the brain's] circuits with pharmacology, you can do it with natural rewards too." As a result of this research, some analysts now believe that behaviors can be as addictive as drugs. They contend that the underlying psychological and physiological processes associated with compulsive behaviors and drug abuse are much the same. Markus explains:

> A significant broadening of the range of activities labeled as addiction resulted from research indicating that compulsive behaviors—in addition to the more commonly acknowledged addictive substances—also result in neurochemical changes. . . . In this view, whether the addiction is to food, substances, sex, gambling, other objects or activities, the characteristics of the addictive process are similar.

Despite these recent research findings, many commentators remain reluctant to expand the concept of addiction to include compulsive behaviors. Part of the reason for this is because a precise definition of addiction remains elusive. Shaffer concludes, "Without more clarity and precision, it will remain difficult to distinguish between someone experiencing an overwhelming impulse to act in a self-destructive way and someone who is simply unwilling to control his or her destructive impulses to act." In *Opposing Viewpoints: Addiction*, this and other controversies surrounding the concept of addiction are debated in the following chapters: Is Addiction a Serious Problem? What Factors Contribute to Addiction? What Are the Most Effective Treatments for Addiction? How Should the Government Deal with Addiction? The authors express diverse views about how addiction should be defined.

CHAPTER 1

Is Addiction a Serious Problem?

Chapter Preface

One of many controversies in the addiction field is whether compulsive behaviors such as excessive gambling and overeating should be considered addictions or simply pathological behavior. Even among those mental health experts who are comfortable viewing many behaviors as addictions, there is strong disagreement about whether sexual compulsivity should be viewed as an addiction. This disagreement even extends to sex experts. Clinical psychologist Dennis P. Sugrue writes, "Few topics in the sexology field have galvanized people into opposing camps as stridently as the topics of sex addiction and sexual compulsivity. They are lightening rods in a 20-year-old controversy about the nature and origin of problematic high-frequency sexual behavior."

Psychologist Patrick Carnes, one of the most fervent supporters of the concept of sex addiction, argues that "during the past three decades, professionals have acknowledged that some people use sex to manage their internal distress. These people are similar to compulsive gamblers, compulsive overeaters, or alcoholics in that they are not able to contain their impulses—and with destructive results." Carnes defines sex addiction as any sexually related, compulsive behavior that interferes with normal living and eventually becomes unmanageable. The most recent edition of the *Diagnostic and Statistical Manual of Mental Disorders* (DSM-IV), published by the American Psychiatric Association, describes addictive disorders such as alcoholism and pathological gambling as having three characteristics: a loss of control, a continuation of the behavior or the use of the substance despite adverse consequences, and a preoccupation with the substance or the behavior. Those who believe that sex addiction should be included in the manual as a mental disorder argue that it fits all of these categories. According to Mark Griffith, who writes for *Psychology Review*,

> Like an alcoholic or a pathological gambler, sexual addicts are unable to stop their self-destructive sexual behavior. In fact, sex addicts will often ignore severe emotional, interpersonal, and physical consequences of their behavior. The consequences of excessive sexual behavior are far-reaching and

can result in losing relationships, family break-ups, difficulties with work, arrests, financial troubles, a loss of interest in things not sexual, low self-esteem and despair. . . . To sex addicts, sex is more important than anything and anyone else and they will engage in the behavior to the neglect of almost everything else.

Other analysts disagree with the premise that excessive sexual behavior is an addiction. According to therapist Marty Klein, publisher of *Sexual Intelligence*, "Most people who self-diagnose as 'sex addicts' aren't compulsive. . . . They're mostly unremarkable people who simply don't like the consequences of their sexual choices—but do not want to deal with the emotional distress that would arise if they made different choices." Another of Klein's concerns is that making sex addiction into a mental disorder implies that sex needs to be controlled, thus declaring sexually healthy people unhealthy. Klein explains:

The sex addiction movement must . . . inevitably say that people are in danger of becoming addicted and thereby lose their ability to make wholesome choices. We're told that at some point something can happen to healthy people—they can, for example, consume a lot of pornography—and they can become addicted. And so everyone's at risk. The sexual addiction diagnostic criteria make problems of non-problematic experiences, and as a result pathologize a majority of people.

Making unpopular sexual practices into mental disorders is nothing new, maintains Klein. "People who advocated birth control in the 1920s were labeled psychiatrically ill. And we all know that frigidity and homosexuality have been labeled psychiatric diseases," Klein contends. He adds: "Sex addiction falls right into this tradition of 'diagnosing' non-conforming sexual expression as disease."

Whether or not compulsive sex should be classified with substance abuse and other excessive behaviors as an addiction disorder remains controversial. The authors of the viewpoints in the following chapter express their opinions on the nature and scope of addiction.

"The Internet is fueling gambling problems, sex addictions and other forms of compulsive behavior."

The Internet Is Fueling Addictions

Brian McCormick

According to Brian McCormick in the following viewpoint, the Internet fuels addictions to sex, gambling, and the Internet itself. The Internet accelerates addictions because of its accessibility, affordability, and anonymity, McCormick claims. Although an increasing number of medical professionals acknowledge that Internet-related addictions are a growing public health problem, contends McCormick, the methods for treating these addicts remains controversial. Brian McCormick is a staff editor for *American Medical News*.

As you read, consider the following questions:
1. What three groups of people access the Internet for sexual gratification, according to research conducted by Al Cooper?
2. In the author's view, what convinced those who treat addicted patients that Internet-related addiction is a problem?
3. In McCormick's opinion, why do most experts say that the tools for treating Internet-related addictions are similar to those used to address other compulsions?

Brian McCormick, "Hooked on the Net," *American Medical News*, vol. 43, June 19, 2000, p. 17. Copyright © 2000 by the American Medical Association. Reproduced by permission.

The Internet is fueling gambling problems, sex addictions and other forms of compulsive behavior. The burgeoning technology also is raising new treatment issues.

A Typical Story

Jarvis, 62, says sexual compulsions have been a problem for most of his life. But his problems intensified two years ago when he discovered sexually explicit chat rooms on the Internet.

"I could lose myself for hours or days without ever leaving home," he said. "The level of isolation and separation from real people was jarring. I had an active real life with friends and a job I loved, but I was spending more and more time in an online fantasy world, which I found ultimately to be a very empty, unsatisfying way to live."

According to . . . research findings, Jarvis is one of more than 100,000—and possibly one of more than 2 million—Internet sex addicts. Another million or more may be developing gambling addictions either exclusively or predominantly online, and several hundred thousand may be developing an unhealthy dependence on the Internet itself.

These findings represent the tip of a new and ominous public health threat, one that to date is basically being ignored, according to those who treat Internet-related addictions and compulsions.

The Cybersex Compulsive

A . . . survey of more than 9,000 Internet users found that 1% of those who visited sex-related sites could be categorically classified as "cybersex compulsives," devoting large amounts of time to the pursuit of sex online and suffering serious consequences as a result. Another 17% were identified as having significant but less severe problems related to sex and the Internet.

Al Cooper, PhD, published the research in a [Spring 2000] special issue of the journal *Sexual Addiction and Compulsivity* devoted to cybersex. His study found three groups of people accessing the Internet for sexual gratification. The first, and largest, were recreational users, for whom it did not seem to be a problem. The second group involved people who already had problems with sexual compulsion that were intensified or exacerbated on the Internet. The third, an at-risk group, were people for whom sexual compulsion would never have been an issue had it not been for the Internet's powerful draw.

Dr. Cooper said that with more than 60 million people on the Internet and at least 20% of that group visiting pornographic sites or engaging in sexually explicit chat, the scope of the problem quickly becomes apparent.

"Using our very conservative definition of a cybersex compulsive, that means at least 120,000 people are suffering from this condition. If the rate of any other disease had gone from virtually zero to 120,000 in five years, it would be declared an epidemic and the full resources of the health system would be brought to bear on it," said Dr. Cooper, clinical director of the San Jose (Calif.) Marital and Sexuality Centre. He also said that while the National Institute of Mental Health is now beginning to look at the issue, the response of the health care community in general has been inadequate.

An Intense Delivery Device

Those who treat addictions related to the Internet have seen a learning curve among their colleagues. "When I first began dealing with this in 1994, everyone laughed about it. There were even tongue-in-cheek articles about the need for 12-step programs to treat Internet addicts," said Kimberly S. Young, PsyD, who in 1995 created the Center for Online Addiction in Bradford, Pa. "Well, no one is laughing now."

Dr. Young treats people for whom the Internet is a means to access compulsions, such as sex and gambling, as well as those who are dependent on the Internet itself.

For many who treat addicted patients, seeing the impact of the Internet firsthand made believers of them. "I've been treating sexually compulsive people for many years, and I've seen the Internet change the landscape in much the same way crack cocaine did for those who treat drug addicts," said Jennifer Schneider, MD, an internist and addiction medicine specialist in Tucson, Ariz. "The computer is an extremely intense delivery device."

Dr. Cooper agrees that the Internet has "turbocharged"

sexual compulsions for many patients, and he attributes the power of the Internet to what he calls the "Triple A" effect: the accessibility, affordability and anonymity of acting out sexually online.

"My wife doesn't give me everything I want, 24 hours a day, seven days a week, but for those who seek sexual gratification through their computers, the Internet can," said Dr. Cooper. And the relatively low cost compared with other forms of acting out, such as strip clubs, prostitutes or phone sex, also eliminates a barrier.

The Influence of Internet Anonymity

But the anonymity of virtual sex may provide its biggest boost. "You can be any gender, race, occupation or age you want to be," said John Sealy, MD, medical director of a full-time inpatient recovery center for sexual addiction at Del Amo Hospital in Torrance, Calif.

Those same factors help to explain why compulsive gamblers are also increasingly turning to the Internet, said Kevin O'Neill, deputy director of the Council on Compulsive Gambling of New Jersey Inc. "For compulsive gamblers, this venue—unlike casinos, riverboats, lotteries or any other form of gambling—is not monitored or regulated," he said. That means gamblers often have no upper-end limit on how much they can lose and can spiral down in their addictions more quickly and severely.

The secrecy of Internet gambling also holds allure for these compulsives, who often have a great deal of shame associated with their behavior, O'Neill said. That helps explain why the number of online casinos and other gaming sites went from about 160 to more than 1,000 last year, and how online gambling has become more than a billion-dollar business [in 2000].

Bev, a 54-year-old recovering alcoholic, says she probably always had a problem with gambling. But it got out of hand only after she discovered online casinos in 1998.

When she lost her job a few months later, she devoted most of her waking time to Internet gambling, maxing out three credit cards, cashing in a 401(k), and nearly destroying a 30-year marriage. With the help of a therapist, medication,

Gamblers Anonymous and online support groups, Bev has been able to refrain from gambling since January [2000].

Dr. Sealy said it is the very isolation of the Internet that both appeals to and eventually entraps addicts. "Addiction is based on isolation and intense loneliness," he said. "These online interactions give the addict the illusion of being connected to counter that loneliness and shame, but ultimately as the medium is abused, it only serves to compound the loneliness and the shame."

Other therapists add that the incidence of cross-addiction seems very prevalent among Internet addicts.

"We began as a chemical dependency treatment center, and we saw that one-third of our patients had gambling problems," said Angie Moore, coordinator of addiction and counseling services at the Illinois Institute for Addiction Recovery at Proctor Hospital in Peoria, Ill.

"As we started treating online gambling addicts, we saw that about one-half of them had chemical dependencies, as well," Moore said.

Treating Internet Addictions

Because it is linked so closely to other addictive behaviors, most experts say the tools for diagnosing and treating Internet-related addictions also are similar to those of other compulsions.

"Patients won't willingly share this information; they have too much shame associated with it," Dr. Sealy said. "Physicians who suspect a problem should ask open-ended questions such as, 'Is there something in your life that feels out of control or that is sapping an inordinate amount of your time and energy?' Most important, doctors need to address this without any hint of shame or judgment. These patients are usually acting out against their own ethics and principles, and they won't open up if they sense the least bit of judgment."

Dr. Schneider adds that for a profession that has repeatedly underdiagnosed and undertreated addiction, changing the average physician's mind-set may be the key to better diagnosis. "Doctors won't know that this is a problem until they know it can be a problem," she said.

Most experts say that, as with other addictions, the preferred treatment includes a combination of therapy and participation in self-help recovery groups. But not all agree with that prescription.

Handelsman. © 1999 by Tribune Media Services. All rights reserved. Reproduced by permission.

"I've found that Internet addicts are not at all receptive to the idea of 12-step recovery groups," Dr. Young said. She has been among the pioneers in another treatment approach, online counseling.

Logging On for Treatment?

"With the opening of my center, I quickly became the Ann Landers of online therapists," Dr. Young said, "and that eventually evolved into online therapy." For $75 an hour, significantly less than her office rates, Dr. Young will treat patients via computer. But that form of treatment has drawn its own detractors.

"I think that ethically, you need to pick up a phone or see a patient in an office setting," O'Neill said. "In addition to being ethically questionable, I don't think it is particularly effective to treat patients with the very tool through which they are dissociating."

Dr. Sealy insists online therapy has both positive and negative aspects. "Many addicts become so isolated that they have no other way of relating. This may provide a method by which they can reach out and seek help. But recovery needs to be experiential. The patient will inevitably need to interact with a therapist and will likely need to be confronted, and neither of those can be accomplished very well via computer."

The role of the computer in the life of a recovering Internet addict is also controversial. Although many therapists say the increasingly ubiquitous Internet will require most patients to find ways to coexist with their computers, much as compulsive overeaters need to learn to eat moderately, others still counsel abstinence from the Web.

"I realize some people believe in controlled Internet use, but some people believe in controlled drinking for alcoholics; we don't," Moore said. "Once the Internet has become a problem, the risks of exposure vastly outweigh the need for that access."

"[That 6 percent of Internet users are addicts] cannot be confidently applied to Internet users in general."

The Threat of Internet Addiction Is Exaggerated

Jacob Sullum

Internet addiction is not a major threat to public health, argues Jacob Sullum in the following viewpoint. Although Internet use, like many pleasurable activities, can for some lead to unhealthy patterns of behavior, claiming that this abuse is an objectively identifiable medical disorder is misleading, Sullum claims. Trying to equate Internet and drug addiction, he asserts, leads people to the conclusion that the problem of Internet addiction is greater than it really is. Jacob Sullum is a senior editor of *Reason*, a magazine that supports individual freedom and opposes big government.

As you read, consider the following questions:
1. According to Sullum, why is psychologist David Greenfield's survey skewed?
2. According to the *Detroit News*, what will happen if Internet addiction is defined as a disorder?
3. In Sullum's opinion, what has Greenfield lost sight of when comparing all pleasurable activities to drug abuse?

Jacob Sullum, "Web Heads," *Reason*, August 25, 1999. Copyright © 1999 by the Reason Foundation. Reproduced by permission of Creators Syndicate.

Journalists never seem to tire of discovering that human beings remain human even when they go online. From gambling and pornography to fraud and pederasty, the Internet makes everything old new again.

In this category of familiar stories with a cyberspace twist, one of the hardiest topics is Internet addiction, which the news media have been warning us about since 1995. The . . . burst of coverage [in 1999] was generated by a study supposedly showing that 6 percent of Internet users are addicts.

The study, presented at the annual meeting of the American Psychological Association (APA), is based on a survey of visitors to ABCNews.com. Among other things, the survey asked them if they felt preoccupied by the Internet, if they used it to escape problems, if they had trouble reducing their online time, and if they lied about the extent of their Internet use.

Psychologist David Greenfield, who developed the survey based on the American Psychiatric Association's diagnostic criteria for "pathological gambling," identified respondents as addicts if they answered yes to five or more such questions. Of the 17,251 people who filled out the survey, 990 met this definition; hence the widely cited "6 percent."

A Limited Sample

Contrary to most of the press coverage, however, this figure cannot be confidently applied to Internet users in general, since the sample was limited to people who happened to visit the ABC News site and who were willing to complete the questionnaire. The fact that ABC News posted the survey in conjunction with its own coverage of Internet addiction probably skewed the sample further.

Some people seem to believe that the true incidence of Internet addiction is not 6 percent but zero. A *Detroit News* editorial called the condition "spurious" and observed, "If it can be successfully defined as a disorder, then Internet addiction will be covered by a good many medical insurance policies, and psychologists can expect a tide of Internet-addicted patients to flow into their offices."

It is hard to ignore the fact that the researchers promoting the concept of Internet addiction tend to be entrepreneurs as well as scientists. Greenfield, a West Hartford, Connecticut, therapist, runs a Web site that offers a "Free Virtual Addiction Test" for people who are wondering if they need professional help.

The Flaws in Internet Addiction Research

The original research into [Internet Addiction Disorder] began with exploratory surveys, which cannot establish *causal* relationships between specific behaviors and their cause. While surveys can help establish descriptions of how people feel about themselves and their behaviors, they cannot draw conclusions about whether a specific technology, such as the Internet, has actually *caused* those behaviors. Those conclusions which are drawn are purely speculative and subjective made by the researchers themselves. Researchers have a name for this logical fallacy, ignoring a common cause. It's one of the oldest fallacies in science, and one still regularly perpetrated in psychological research today.

John M. Grohol, *Internet Addiction Guide*, February 1999.

Psychologist Kimberly Young, who also presented a paper on Internet addiction at the APA meeting, is the founder and CEO of the Center for On-Line Addiction in Bradford, Pennsylvania. She runs the Web site netaddiction.com and offers online counseling to cyberspace junkies at a rate of $55 for each 50-minute session.

But the fact that people make money by "treating" Internet addiction does not mean that the problem is imaginary. After all, no one is forced to ask Greenfield or Young for help in controlling his Internet use.

An Unhealthy Pattern of Behavior

Some people, by their own judgment, spend too much time online, jeopardizing their work, their health, or their relationships with family and friends. To insist that such a damaging preoccupation is not really an addiction because it does not involve a drug is to insist on an arbitrarily narrow definition that ignores everyday experience.

In real life, people can develop strong attachments to all sorts of things: food, sex, exercise, gambling, shopping, TV, video games. Sometimes these attachments get out of hand.

This is what we mean when we talk about addiction: a pattern of behavior, not a chemical reaction.

When psychiatrists talk about addiction, by contrast, they pretend they are dealing with a precisely defined, objectively verifiable medical disorder. And when Greenfield urges them to recognize Internet addiction as such a disorder, he mimics their biological reductionism.

"The underlying neurochemical changes that occur during any pleasurable act have proven themselves to be potentially addictive on a brain-behavior level," he writes. But notice what this means: Any source of pleasure can be the focus of an addiction.

Greenfield loses sight of the point that drug abuse is simply one form of addiction, instead treating it as a template that all genuine addictions have to match. In his eagerness to show that the Internet is just like a drug, he calls it "potent," emphasizes "tolerance and withdrawal symptoms," and draws an analogy between higher modem speeds and faster routes of drug administration.

"There's a power here that's different from anything we've dealt with before," Greenfield declared at the APA meeting. Here is yet another way in which the Internet resembles drugs: Both inspire exaggeration.

"Most smokers use tobacco regularly because they are addicted to nicotine."

Nicotine Addiction Harms Society

National Institute on Drug Abuse

In the following viewpoint the National Institute on Drug Abuse (NIDA) argues that most people smoke tobacco products because they are addicted to nicotine. According to NIDA, research shows that nicotine increases the levels of dopamine in the brain, which triggers feelings of pleasure, thus encouraging users to continue nicotine use. Tobacco smoking is responsible for more than four hundred thousand deaths in the United States each year and $138 billion in health care costs, NIDA claims. NIDA is an agency of the National Institutes of Health.

As you read, consider the following questions:
1. In NIDA's view, how is nicotine absorbed by the body?
2. According to NIDA, what led scientists to believe that nicotine might not be the only psychoactive ingredient in tobacco?
3. What did the 1999 National Household Survey on Drug Abuse reveal about adolescent smoking habits?

National Institute on Drug Abuse, "Nicotine Addiction," www.nida.nih.gov, 2002.

Nicotine, one of more than 4,000 chemicals found in the smoke from tobacco products such as cigarettes, cigars, and pipes, is the primary component in tobacco that acts on the brain. Smokeless tobacco products such as snuff and chewing tobacco also contain many toxins as well as high levels of nicotine. Nicotine, recognized as one of the most frequently used addictive drugs, is a naturally occurring colorless liquid that turns brown when burned and acquires the odor of tobacco when exposed to air. There are many species of tobacco plants; the tabacum species serves as the major source of tobacco products today. Since nicotine was first identified in the early 1800s, it has been studied extensively and shown to have a number of complex and sometimes unpredictable effects on the brain and the body.

Cigarette smoking is the most prevalent form of nicotine addiction in the United States. Most cigarettes in the U.S. market today contain 10 milligrams (mg) or more of nicotine. Through inhaling smoke, the average smoker takes in 1 to 2 mg nicotine per cigarette. There have been substantial increases in the sale and consumption of smokeless tobacco products also, and more recently, in cigar sales.

Nicotine is absorbed through the skin and mucosal lining of the mouth and nose or by inhalation in the lungs. Depending on how tobacco is taken, nicotine can reach peak levels in the bloodstream and brain rapidly. Cigarette smoking, for example, results in rapid distribution of nicotine throughout the body, reaching the brain within 10 seconds of inhalation. Cigar and pipe smokers, on the other hand, typically do not inhale the smoke, so nicotine is absorbed more slowly through the mucosal membranes of their mouths. Nicotine from smokeless tobacco also is absorbed through the mucosal membranes.

Is Nicotine Addictive?

Yes, nicotine is addictive. Most smokers use tobacco regularly because they are addicted to nicotine. Addiction is characterized by compulsive drug-seeking and use, even in the face of negative health consequences, and tobacco use certainly fits the description. It is well documented that most smokers identify tobacco as harmful and express a desire to reduce or stop using it, and nearly 35 million of them make a serious attempt to quit each year. Unfortunately, less than 7 percent of those who try to quit on their own achieve more than 1 year of abstinence; most relapse within a few days of attempting to quit.

Other factors to consider besides nicotine's addictive properties include its high level of availability, the small number of legal and social consequences of tobacco use, and the sophisticated marketing and advertising methods used by tobacco companies. These factors, combined with nicotine's addictive properties, often serve as determinants for first use and, ultimately, addiction.

Trends in Teen Smoking

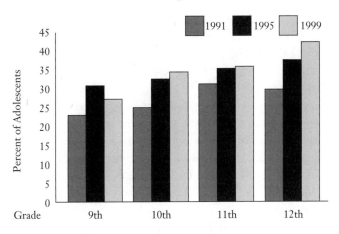

Centers for Disease Control and Prevention, 2000.

Nicotine and the Brain

Research has shown in fine detail how nicotine acts on the brain to produce a number of behavioral effects. Of primary importance to its addictive nature are findings that nicotine activates the brain circuitry that regulates feelings of pleasure, the so-called reward pathways. A key brain chemical involved in mediating the desire to consume drugs is the neurotransmitter dopamine, and research has shown that nicotine increases the levels of dopamine in the reward circuits. Nicotine's pharmacokinetic properties have been found also to enhance its abuse potential. Cigarette smoking produces a rapid distribution of nicotine to the brain, with drug levels peaking within 10 seconds of inhalation. The acute effects of nicotine dissipate in a few minutes, causing the smoker to continue dosing frequently throughout the day to maintain the drug's pleasurable effects and prevent withdrawal.

What people frequently do not realize is that the cigarette is a very efficient and highly engineered drug-delivery system. By inhaling, the smoker can get nicotine to the brain very rapidly with every puff. A typical smoker will take 10 puffs on a cigarette over a period of 5 minutes that the cigarette is lit. Thus, a person who smokes about 1-1/2 packs (30 cigarettes) daily, gets 300 "hits" of nicotine to the brain each day. These factors contribute considerably to nicotine's highly addictive nature.

Scientific research is also beginning to show that nicotine may not be the only psychoactive ingredient in tobacco. Using advanced neuroimaging technology, scientists can see the dramatic effect of cigarette smoking on the brain and are finding a marked decrease in the levels of monoamineoxidase (MAO), an important enzyme that is responsible for breaking down dopamine. The change in MAO must be caused by some tobacco smoke ingredient other than nicotine, since we know that nicotine itself does not dramatically alter MAO levels. The decrease in two forms of MAO, A and B, then results in higher dopamine levels and may be another reason that smokers continue to smoke—to sustain the high dopamine levels that result in the desire for repeated drug use.

What Is the Impact of Tobacco Use?

According to the 1999 National Household Survey on Drug Abuse, an estimated 57.0 million Americans were current smokers and 7.6 million used smokeless tobacco, which means that nicotine is one of the most widely abused substances. In addition, in 1998 each day in the United States more than 2,000 people under the age of 18 began daily smoking. According to the Centers for Disease Control and Prevention (CDC), the prevalence of cigarette smoking among U.S. high school students increased from 27.5 percent in 1991 to 36.4 percent in 1997 before declining to 34.8 percent in 1999. NIDA's [National Institute on Drug Abuse] own Monitoring the Future Study, which annually surveys drug use and related attitudes of America's adolescents, also found the prevalence rates for smoking among youth declined from 1999 to 2000. Since 1975, nicotine in the form of cigarettes has consistently been the substance the greatest number of high school students use daily.

The impact of nicotine addiction in terms of morbidity, mortality, and economic costs to society is staggering. Tobacco kills more than 430,000 U.S. citizens each year—more than alcohol, cocaine, heroin, homicide, suicide, car accidents, fire, and AIDS combined. Tobacco use is the leading preventable cause of death in the United States.

Economically, an estimated $80 billion of total U.S. health care costs each year is attributable to smoking. However, this cost is well below the total cost to society because it does not include burn care from smoking-related fires, perinatal care for low-birth-weight infants of mothers who smoke, and medical care costs associated with disease caused by secondhand smoke. Taken together, the direct and indirect costs of smoking are estimated at $138 billion per year.

4

"The notion that nicotine is an addictive substance lacks reasonable empirical support."

The Addictive Properties of Nicotine Are Unproven

Dale M. Atrens

While most people assume that nicotine is addictive, research on nicotine addiction does not support this assumption, argues Dale M. Atrens in the following viewpoint. Nicotine does not meet the criteria that defines addiction, Atrens claims. He maintains, for example, that one element of the Surgeon General's definition for addiction—that addiction takes precedence over other important priorities in the lives of addicts—does not apply to nicotine; most smokers have no problem not smoking in situations where laws prohibit smoking, for example. Atrens, author of *The Neurosciences and Behavior*, is a lecturer in psychobiology at the University of Sydney, in Australia.

As you read, consider the following questions:
1. According to Atrens, what two factors compromise the verbal reports of drug users?
2. What broad behaviors have been labeled "addictions," according to the author?
3. In Atrens's opinion, what is the most serious deficiency in using animal models to study human drug taking?

Dale M. Atrens, "Nicotine as an Addictive Substance: A Critical Examination of the Basic Concepts and Empirical Evidence," *Journal of Drug Issues*, vol. 31, June 9, 2001, pp. 87–114. Copyright © 2001 by *Journal of Drug Issues*. Reproduced by permission.

The addiction model has dominated smoking research for over a generation. Tobacco smoke is said to contain numerous agents that cause ill health as well as a powerful addictive drug, nicotine. According to the dominant model, as the nicotine addiction develops, the smoker becomes progressively less able to stop. The essence of the nicotine addiction hypothesis is that smokers are unable to stop because nicotine changes the brain in such a way as to perpetuate its use. More broadly, drug addictions are seen as representing brain dysfunctions. . . .

A Common View

The 1988 Surgeon General's Report on Smoking and Health states the nicotine addiction viewpoint succinctly:

> Cigarettes and other forms of tobacco are addicting. Nicotine is the drug in tobacco that causes addiction. The pharmacologic and behavioral processes that determine tobacco addiction are similar to those that determine addiction to drugs such as heroin and cocaine. . . .

It is nearly impossible to find a contemporary document on smoking that doesn't mention nicotine addiction as an incontestable point in the first paragraph. Many believe that the recent admissions of tobacco companies constitute further proof that nicotine is addictive. This belief is peculiar since the earlier denials of the tobacco companies were widely held to be false and self-serving. The validity of the nicotine addiction hypothesis is not about admissions, assertions, or concessions; it is about logic and data.

Questioning the Addiction Model

With sufficient use, certain drugs are said to change the brain in such a way as to make cessation difficult or impossible. Drug users frequently state that they cannot help themselves. The nature of this alleged helplessness remains unclear. Drugs such as opiates and cocaine are clearly very enjoyable, and users often report that such drugs produce intense feelings of pleasure. It is possible that intense pleasure could account for persistent drug use. On the other hand, drugs such as nicotine have only small and variable subjective effects. Although smoking may be pleasant, the effects are not at all comparable to traditional drugs of abuse. Nicotine's lack of potent subjective effects necessitates some other sort of mechanism to account for persistent use. This other mechanism requires a unique pharmacological property, a pleasure-independent ability to lead the user into repeated use. However, at the moment there is no evidence of any neural mechanisms that could mediate such an unprecedented effect.

The most direct form of evidence supporting the belief that drugs induce a form of helplessness in certain users is the verbal reports of the users themselves. That users may not stop is obvious; whether they cannot stop is another matter. The utility of the verbal reports of drug users is compromised by at least two major factors. Drug users, including smokers, tend to suffer from diverse forms of psychopathology. Thus, even with the best of intentions, the fidelity of their verbal reports is uncertain. However, drug users often do not have good intentions. They tend to explain their behavior in a manner that minimizes personal responsibility. This has clear social and legal advantages. Such considerations suggest that the verbal reports of drug users may not be valid explanations of their behavior. Such reports are, at best, pre-scientific data. . . .

The addiction model is counterproductive to the aim of reducing problem drug use. Since its ascendancy there has been little progress made in the treatment of drug taking. In spite of a plethora of theory, research, and application, the success rate for treating common drug problems is so poor that it is rarely mentioned in scientific reports. In contrast, some 50 million Americans alone have quit smoking.

The main reason given by smokers for their failure to stop smoking is that they see themselves as addicted. Smokers are widely portrayed as victims of rogue molecular processes in their brains. As long as smoking is portrayed as an inexorable addictive process, the success of cessation programs will be limited by a self-fulfilling prophecy.

Defining Addiction

Addiction and related terms have such broad and variable usage that they can mean almost anything. Addiction is used to describe behaviors ranging from injecting heroin and cocaine, to smoking or chewing tobacco, drinking coffee, eating chocolate, shopping, watching television soap operas, and falling in love. There are reports of addiction to water, cardiac defibrillators, carrots, hormone replacement therapy, and numerous other unusual entities. The clinical literature is replete with examples of people who develop unfortunate, even destructive, relationships with a great many substances, objects, events, and people. It is questionable whether these problems are illuminated by invoking the concept of addiction. . . .

Addiction is commonly used to describe drug problems. There can be little objection to such loose everyday use of addiction. The difficulties arise when addiction is used to *explain* drug problems. There is a persistent tendency to confuse description with explanation. There are substantial difficulties even when addiction is used in a descriptive sense. However, there are still greater difficulties when addiction is used to explain persistent drug use. . . .

Examining the Surgeon General's Definition

The Surgeon General's definition states that "the user's behavior is largely controlled by a psychoactive substance." Whereas nicotine certainly affects behavior, it is questionable whether it can properly be said to control behavior. It has yet to be demonstrated that nicotine can exert more control over behavior than that exerted by any of scores of innocuous substances and events. Moreover, smoking is almost always done along with something else. The fact that smoking enhances a broad range of abilities suggests that the user's behavior is *not* controlled by the substance. In this context the behavioral consequences of nicotine are little different from those of eating a carrot.

Although the Surgeon General stresses that an addiction "takes precedence over other important priorities," this rarely applies to smoking. The overwhelming majority of smokers know when they can and cannot smoke, and they usually find increasingly severe restrictions only a minor nuisance. Certain religions prohibit smoking on the Sabbath, and even the heaviest smokers report no difficulty in observing this rule. It is difficult to imagine a molecular dysfunction of the brain that respects the Sabbath.

The Surgeon General stresses that addictive substances are reinforcing (rewarding). . . . At best, nicotine may be slightly more rewarding than saline. Even under the most carefully contrived circumstances, nicotine is probably no more rewarding than a flash of light or a brief sound. Such feeble reward does not suggest abuse potential. . . .

Next the Surgeon General's definition refers to the substance use continuing: ". . . despite damage to the individual or to society." However, smoking produces no damage in many people and most smokers respond to danger signs by stopping. Few people with clear signs of smoking-related illness persist in smoking; they are not representative of smokers in general.

An Inadequate Concept

The notion of nicotine addiction suffers from numerous and major conceptual, definitional, and empirical inadequacies. Some reflect general problems with the concept of addiction, whereas others are specific to nicotine.

A recurring source of difficulty for the nicotine addiction hypothesis is the continuing lack of consensus concerning a definition of addiction. Hundreds of definitions have been offered, yet none withstands any scrutiny. Rigorous definitions of addiction clearly exclude nicotine, whereas those that reasonably include nicotine also include so many other substances and events that the notion of addiction becomes trivialized.

Lacking a reasonable definition of addiction, the putative addictiveness of drugs has become a matter of legislative fiat, judicial rulings, and committee edicts. Not surprisingly, which drugs are considered addictive varies markedly over time and in different places. Cannabis was long considered to be the scourge of our youth while tobacco was considered relatively harmless. Recently this position has been reversed. This is not science, but politics.

Self-administration studies, [in which lab animals press a bar to receive a drug or other stimulus] in laboratory species are said to support the view that nicotine, much like heroin and cocaine, is powerfully reinforcing. However, nicotine self-administration doesn't remotely approach the vigor or reliability of that supported by drugs such as cocaine and heroin. The strongest reinforcing effects of nicotine in laboratory species are less than those of innocuous reinforcers such as light, sound, sugar, or salt.

Moreover, nicotine self-administration requires doses that are far higher than humans ever encounter. These effects may well represent monoaminergic effects of high nicotine doses. There are no reports of nicotine self-administration in laboratory species at doses even approaching those self-administered by humans. It is unjustified to use weak and inconsistent reinforcement effects obtained with high intravenous doses in laboratory species as evidence for human abuse potential.

Perhaps the most serious deficiency in using animal models to study human drug taking is that animals do not seem to get 'hooked' on any substance. This is particularly true of nicotine. It is difficult to show any rewarding effects of nicotine in laboratory species, let alone the powerful effects associated with drugs of abuse. It is possible that drug abuse is a uniquely human phenomenon.

What Is the Active Ingredient in Smoke?

It is not universally accepted . . . that nicotine is the active ingredient in tobacco smoke. The authors of the widely respected "Merck Manual" say only that it is "probably" the active ingredient. If, in fact, the anti-smokers finally succeed in getting the tobacco companies to remove the nicotine from cigarettes, we will finally find out the truth. My own bet is that a cigarette without nicotine will probably be almost as satisfying as one with nicotine. The active ingredient in smoke is smoke.

Lauren A. Colby, *In Defense of Smokers*, 1999.

Like the data from animal experimentation, the data on nicotine reinforcement in humans do not suggest that nicotine has abuse potential. There are no credible demonstrations in humans that nicotine is any more reinforcing than many other substances and events that have no abuse potential. The subjective effects of nicotine suggest a drug that is pleasant, nothing more. In this crucial respect, nicotine contrasts markedly with reference drugs such as cocaine and heroin that consistently produce strong feelings of euphoria.

Addiction Is Not a Brain Disease

There have been attempts to lend credibility to the notion of addiction by describing it as a brain disease. However, there is little evidence for such a view. There is no special brain state associated with nicotine use. Although nicotine has diverse effects on the brain, none has any significant potential to perpetuate nicotine use. Moreover, the neural effects of nicotine and other putatively addictive drugs are indistinguishable from those produced by many relatively harmless substances and everyday experiences.

Nicotine has effects on dopaminergic transmission that, in certain respects, resemble those of cocaine or heroin. However, almost anything that alters arousal alters dopaminergic transmission. Such neurochemical effects should not be interpreted as a correlate of addiction. The fact that some of the effects on dopamine transmission may be restricted to the shell of the nucleus accumbens is interesting, but irrelevant to whether nicotine or anything else is addictive.

The finding that dopamine may be involved in the effects of nicotine and reinforcement processes lends no support to the notion that nicotine is addictive. The dopamine hypothesis of reinforcement remains an intensely debated issue in which the theory, methodology, and empirical findings are all disputed. Claims to the contrary notwithstanding, none of the many variants of the dopamine theory has, as yet, any implications for human drug use. There is no justification for making the major leap from the poorly understood neural sequelae of reinforcement in laboratory species to the still more poorly defined and understood notion of addiction in humans.

The effects of nicotine, like those of virtually every other drug, psychoactive or not, show a degree of tolerance. It is questionable whether this ubiquitous phenomenon says anything about abuse potential. It certainly does not distinguish nicotine from many other innocuous substances.

Nicotine use may sometimes produce withdrawal effects. However, many drugs with no abuse potential produce withdrawal effects that are much more dramatic than those produced by nicotine. Conversely, many drugs with substantial abuse potential produce little in the way of withdrawal effects. Additionally, nicotine withdrawal effects last for no more than a few weeks, whereas relapse potential may last for years. The fact that withdrawal and relapse potential have such different temporal characteristics indicates that they cannot be causally related.

In summary, apart from numerous conceptual and definitional inadequacies, the notion that nicotine is an addictive substance lacks reasonable empirical support. There are so many and such grossly conflicting findings that adhering to the nicotine addiction thesis is only defensible on political, not scientific, grounds. More broadly, addiction may have some use as a description of certain types of behavior, but it fails badly as an explanation of such behaviors.

It is commonly assumed that questioning the addiction hypothesis is to condone and even advocate drug use. Such an assumption is incorrect. In order to develop effective treatments for drug problems, it is necessary to escape from the unproductive ideology that is currently dominant. Abandoning the concept of addiction is a step in this direction.

"*Legalized gambling destroys individuals and families, increases crime and ultimately costs society far more than the government makes.*"

Compulsive Gambling Is a National Concern

Tom Grey

In the following viewpoint Tom Grey argues that compulsive gambling has become a national epidemic. Once illegal in all states but Nevada, legalized gambling has grown as governments have come to see the revenues they receive from state-sponsored and state-sanctioned gambling as a means to balance state budgets and promote economic growth, claims Grey. However, gambling addiction destroys individuals and their families as well as increases crime in communities that have legalized gambling, Grey maintains. The price society pays for compulsive gambling, he argues, far outweighs any revenue governments may gain from it. Grey, a Methodist minister, is executive director of the National Coalition Against Legalized Gambling.

As you read, consider the following questions:
1. What effect did legalization of riverboat casinos have in Iowa, according to Grey?
2. What impact does pathological gambling have on families, in the author's view?
3. According to Earl Grinols, what percentage of a casino's revenues comes from gambling addicts?

Tom Grey, "An Epidemic of Gambling," *Family Voice*, July/August 1999, pp. 16–19. Copyright © 1999 by Concerned Women for America. Reproduced by permission.

Just 18 years old, Bob Hafemann won $500 from an Oregon lottery scratch ticket. He became a regular lottery player, but Bob seemed to have his gambling under control—until Oregon introduced video poker in 1992. Though he earned $45,000 a year, Bob began borrowing money to feed his gambling habit. Then he sold his possessions and stopped paying all his bills but the rent. Utterly destroyed by video gambling, Bob took his own life at age 28. "The gambling addiction completely changed who he was," said Bob's sister.

Legalized gambling not only changes individuals, it changes society. We destroyed Bob—and millions of others—because our governments push a highly addictive activity: gambling. Governments spend millions of dollars warning us about narcotics, alcohol and tobacco, and the campaigns have been effective.

But today, gambling is the fastest growing addiction in America. According to [a June 1999] report of the National Gambling Impact Study Commission (NGISC), about five million pathological and problem gamblers live in America. An additional fifteen million risk developing this addiction.

Besides individuals, state governments have become addicted to the revenues derived from casinos, slot machines, keno and lotto. So instead of warning citizens, many governments exploit them. Ignoring the social costs of gambling, they think the cash will help balance their budgets.

A Gambling Boom

In 1977, every state except Nevada prohibited commercial gambling casinos. Only 13 states had lotteries. Native American casinos didn't exist. All together, Americans wagered about $17 billion on legal commercial gambling.

Between 1976 and 1988, Atlantic City legalized casinos, and the number of state lotteries more than doubled. By 1994, 21 new states had legalized gambling casinos, and slot or video poker machines were authorized at racetracks and bars in 10 states.

Americans wagered over $600 billion on legal gambling last year—an astonishing 3,500 percent increase in just two decades.

Since mid-1994, anti-gambling activists have nearly halted the expansion of gambling. But the damage has been done.

For 10 years, lawmakers have forgotten why gambling was considered a "vice." But the growth in gambling has sparked research. Today, considerable evidence demonstrates that legalized gambling destroys individuals and families, increases crime and ultimately costs society far more than the government makes.

Gambling addiction is just as real and tragic as alcohol or drug addiction. The American Psychiatric Association and the American Medical Association both recognize pathological (or "compulsive") gambling as a mental disorder.

Experts say that pathological gambling is closely linked to the accessibility and acceptability of gambling. Like alcoholism, only a small percentage of Americans are susceptible. But more legalized gambling exposes more of those prone to addiction. Fast-paced gambling, like casinos and video gambling, also maximizes addiction.

In Iowa, the 1991 legalization of riverboat casinos more than tripled addiction. A study released in 1995 found that 5.4 percent of the state's adults were pathological or problem gamblers—compared to only 1.7 percent before riverboats came.

Just four years after Louisiana legalized casinos and slot machines, a study found that 7 percent of adults had become addicted. In Minnesota, as 16 Indian casinos opened across the state, the number of Gamblers Anonymous groups shot up from 1 to 49.

The Nature of the Problem

Pathological gamblers lose all their money. Then they run up credit card debt. They sell or pawn possessions and beg for loans.

The average Gamblers Anonymous member will have lost all his money and accumulated debts from $35,000 to $92,000 before he seeks treatment. Thousands file bankruptcy. Many commit suicide.

Pathological gambling rarely affects just one person. Families lose savings, college and retirement funds. They suffer foreclosed mortgages. Under the stress, many problem gamblers commit domestic and child abuse. After casinos came to the Mississippi Gulf Coast, domestic violence

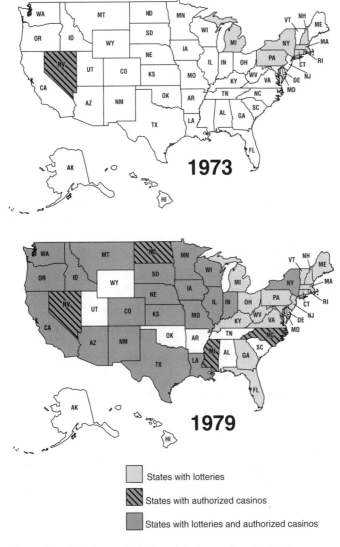

The Increase in Lottery and Casino Gambling

1973

1979

☐ States with lotteries

▨ States with authorized casinos

▨ States with lotteries and authorized casinos

National Gambling Impact Study Commission Report, June 18, 1999.

increased 69 percent. An estimated 37 percent of all pathological gamblers have abused their children.

Many studies support the link between gambling and
crime. But less publicized is how gambling addiction turns
people into criminals. More than half of all pathological

gamblers will commit crimes—embezzlement, tax evasion, fraud—to pay off debts.

The Florida Office of Planning and Budgeting researched projected costs of legalizing casino gambling in the state. The largest potential government expense came from incarcerating new gamblers who turn to crime. According to the study, this "could cost Florida residents *$6.08 billion* [emphasis added]."

The managers of gambling establishments who see these addicts daily should understand.

In Atlantic City, for example, after pathological gamblers lose their cash and empty their ATM accounts, they walk outside to sell their valuables.

About three dozen "Cash for Gold" stores operate near the boardwalk casinos. How many thousands of people are needed each year to keep three dozen "Cash for Gold" stores in business? And why don't the Atlantic City casinos try to help these customers?

Before the U.S. House Judiciary Committee, Professor Earl Grinols of the University of Illinois presented evidence that the casinos depend on addicts for much of their profits. These gamblers represent only 4 percent of adults, but they may account for as much as 52 percent of a casino's revenues.

Similarly, the NGISC's study estimates that 51 percent of all state lottery revenues come from just 5 percent of lottery players.

Gambling Politics

As dreams of prosperity evaporated, state and local citizen groups sprang up to oppose gambling's spread. In 1994, they created the National Coalition Against Legalized Gambling (NCALG).

The members of NCALG span the political spectrum, with activists in every state. They battle gambling's expansion because it harms individuals, families, businesses and society. Despite furious efforts by gambling promoters, [few states have] legalized casinos or slot machines.

The political tide is turning.

[In the summer of 1999], the National Gambling Impact Study Commission issued its report: gambling is out of control. The Commission condemned nearly every type of gambling considered in Congress and state legislatures.

The Commission urged state lotteries to stop preying on the poor. And it challenged Congress to stop Internet gambling, ban gambling "cruises to nowhere," and scrutinize tribal gambling operations.

The report clearly states that gambling is not just recreation. It is addictive and potentially destructive. In fact, the Commission called on schools from elementary levels through college to teach and warn students of gambling's dangers.

Will America continue to belittle the epidemic of gambling addiction? Or will we finally acknowledge that it has become a public health emergency?

All bets are off.

> "*People who have visited casinos and played the lottery have seen that misery and damnation don't necessarily follow.*"

The Dangers of Compulsive Gambling Are Exaggerated

Steve Chapman

In the following viewpoint Steve Chapman refutes claims that legalized gambling is destroying lives and corrupting American communities. For example, those who oppose gambling claim that legalized gambling increases suicide and crime rates, Chapman claims. He asserts, however, that these claims are unfounded; while suicide and crime rates may have risen in some states that have legalized gambling, they have decreased in others, suggesting other factors may be responsible for the increases. Moreover, most people who patronize gambling establishments gamble responsibly; in fact, he argues, only 1.6 percent of American adults will be become gambling addicts. Chapman is a columnist for the *Chicago Tribune*.

As you read, consider the following questions:
1. According to Chapman, what percentage of American adults will become pathological gamblers?
2. How does Chapman refute the argument that gambling depletes the local economy?
3. How does Chapman refute the assumption that gamblers are being fooled?

Steve Chapman, "Vice Is Nice," *Slate*, September 18, 1998. Copyright © 1998 by *Slate*/Distributed by United Feature Syndicate, Inc. Reproduced by permission.

[C] onservative columnist] William Safire and [*New York Times* columnist] Frank Rich hail from opposite ends of the political spectrum, but on the subject of gambling, you could barely squeeze a poker chip between them. Safire preaches his immovable conviction "that casino operators are predators; that state-sponsored lotteries make a mockery of public policy; that politicians who are on the take from gambling interests are wallowing in the occasion of sin." Counterpoint, Frank? ". . .The stench of influence-peddling suffuses some state governments where gambling rules. In the Midwest, riverboat casinos can be an economic boon but sometimes suck local retail businesses dry. Statistics suggest that crime, domestic abuse and alcoholism rise in gambling's wake—while the poor most conspicuously get poorer."

Legal gambling brings out the latent puritan in many Americans. The right detests gambling because it promises something for nothing. The left hates it because it enriches corporations by emptying the pockets of the gullible lower classes. Republican right leader Ralph Reed and the more-liberal-than-thou Harvard political scientist Michael Sandel condemn it, as do [consumer advocate] Ralph Nader and [family values advocate] Gary Bauer.

Everyone seems to detest legal gambling—everyone, that is, except the public. Once regarded as a low habit, gambling is now generally treated as wholesome entertainment in all states but two. Americans spend nearly $51 billion a year on various games of chance—twice as much as they spend on movies, plays, operas, and spectator sports combined.

But gambling's place at the table is threatened by the puritans, who've used their political muscle to help establish a National Gambling Impact Study Commission. They hope its June 1999 report will prove their claims that gambling wrecks lives, stimulates crime, saps local economies, mercilessly exploits human weakness, and sustains itself through bribery and corruption. A review, then, and a brief refutation of their best arguments.

People Become Addicted to Gambling: The critics warn of an exploding epidemic of addicted gamblers, but a recent study by researchers at Harvard Medical School's Division on Addictions argues against this notion. An estimated 1.6

percent of American adults will become pathological gamblers, compared with 6.2 percent who will succumb to drug addiction and 13.8 percent who will become alcoholics. A study published [in 1997] claimed that the legalization of casinos causes an increase in suicide rates. Indeed, Nevada's suicide rate is the highest in the country, double the national average. But New Jersey, home of Atlantic City, enjoys the lowest rate. Mississippi, the South's gambling Mecca, falls slightly below the national average.

Legal Gambling Fosters Crime: Exhibit A for the prosecution is Atlantic City, which went from being No. 50 among American cities in crimes per capita to being No. 1 after the arrival of casinos. This increase fails to account for the city's huge influx of tourists, who on any given day outnumber residents by more than 2-to-1. As noted in a study by University of Maryland Professor Peter Reuter, homicides barely increased at all, despite the influx of outsiders, and assaults rose only about as fast as the average daily population. The real increases have come in robbery and aggravated assaults. Elsewhere, though, it's impossible to detect any consistent relationship between the existence of casinos and the prevalence of lawlessness. Jeremy Margolis, who headed the Illinois State Police when the state introduced 13 riverboat casinos, has testified that "crime has not been a problem." Looking at rural Colorado, Texas A&M scholar Patricia Stokowski found that with the arrival of casinos, "the likelihood of becoming a crime victim in Gilpin County has decreased."

Legal Gambling Depletes the Local Economy: Economists normally extol anything that allows consumers to satisfy their preferences, but several members of the profession depict casinos as the enemy of prosperity. Earl Grinols of the University of Illinois excoriates them as "a shell game, attracting dollars from one person's pocket to another and from one region to another." Another view holds that life for the casinos means death for restaurants, car dealers, hardware stores, and other wholesome businesses unless legal gambling attracts massive numbers of new tourists.

But these are the wrong measures of the economic value of gambling establishments. Existing businesses are threatened when a new business comes to town, whether it's Nordstrom or a shoe repair shop. No economist with ambitions for tenure would dream of dismissing a business as a "shell game" merely because its revenue diverts revenue from other businesses.

A Lack of Evidence

There is no evidence that gamblers are any more likely than nongamblers to forsake responsibility. Indeed, one Swedish study found no relationship between gambling and crime, marital instability, or "the degree of participation in community activities." In another survey, the economist Reuven Brenner of McGill University notes that there is "little evidence to support the view that the majority of gamblers squander their money recklessly, whether it is money spent on stakes or money earned from winnings."

Guy Calvert, *Policy Analysis*, June 18, 1999.

Legal Gambling Causes Corruption: Casino operators are portrayed as the Typhoid Marys [people from whom something undesirable spreads] of political corruption, the usual evidence being their lavish bankrolling of politicians. But of the 16 industries that gave "soft money" to the two major political parties in 1996, the gambling industry ranked 16th, according to the ultrafastidious Center for Responsive Politics.

Casino owners are right to take a greater-than-average interest in the workings of government. 1) Until recently, their industry was illegal almost everywhere. 2) They cannot operate without hard-to-get government licenses. 3) Their many enemies want to legislate them out of existence.

As long as we're talking about corruption and exploitation, we should not forget that the wickedest gambling sharpies don't live in Las Vegas but in the state capitals, where the lotteries are headquartered. The lotteries' pitiful payout—about half of all money wagered, compared with 92 percent or so at your average casino—rightly draws cries of outrage. If the critics were interested in remedying the lotteries, they'd have the states repeal their monopolies on these games and let the market compete away the excess profits.

Whose Life Is It, Anyway? Gambling's opponents never tire of reciting statistics and anecdotes to suggest that the costs of legalized gambling dwarf any possible benefits. But they fail to count the central benefit—the diversion and pleasure it provides to millions of people. Until 1978, casinos were accessible only to people with the means to travel to Las Vegas. The relaxation of prohibitionist laws has brought them within easy reach of most of the American public, and the public has voted for them with its feet. The overwhelming majority of these patrons gamble responsibly and impose no burden on their fellow citizens. They treat games of chance as exactly that—games.

Yet critics insist on portraying gamblers as a pitiable class of suckers, enslaved by fantasies of unearned wealth. It's hard to see why. No one accuses movie theaters or gardening-supply outlets of ruthlessly exploiting the weaknesses of clients who turn over their money only because they lack the self-control to refuse. Most people who patronize the lottery, the track, or the slot machines end up poorer, with nothing to show for the transaction—which is also true of people who eat in restaurants and attend concerts. To incurable bluenoses, gambling is an infuriating scam. But why assume gamblers are being fooled? It's more reasonable to assume that they know they will probably lose but are happy to take that chance for 1) the pleasure of playing and 2) the chance of coming out ahead.

In the end, that's a decision they ought to be free to make, unimpeded by moralists and social reformers who think ordinary people cannot be trusted to look after their own interests. If gambling were the grim scourge portrayed by its opponents, it would not have gone from a contemptible vice to an innocent diversion in a single generation. People who have visited casinos and played the lottery have seen that misery and damnation don't necessarily follow, either for themselves or for surrounding communities. Gambling has become a widespread pastime for the simple and unassailable reason that it adds to the sum of human happiness. That's reason enough to leave it alone.

Periodical Bibliography

The following articles have been selected to supplement the diverse views presented in this chapter.

Dan Allsup	"Gambling's Dark Side," *American Legion*, June 2002.
American Medical Association	"Underage Drinkers' Risk of Brain Damage," *USA Today Magazine*, February 2003.
Karen Asp	"Addicted to Sweat," *American Fitness*, November 1999.
Steven Belenko et al.	"Substance Abuse and the Prison Population," *Corrections Today*, October 1998.
B. Bower	"Youthful Nicotine Addiction May Be Growing," *Science News*, September 22, 2001.
Susan Brink	"When Being First Isn't Best," *U.S. News & World Report*, May 7, 2001.
Thomas E. Broffman	"Why Women Gamble: The Causes and Treatment," *Counselor*, August 2001.
Beth Fontenot	"Consuming Disorders," *Priorities for Health*, 1999.
Mark Griffith	"Addicted to Love? The Psychology of Sex Addiction," *Psychology Review*, November 2001.
Jerome D. Levin	"Sexual Addiction," *National Forum*, Fall 1999.
Mary Lord	"Drinking: Here's Looking at You, Kids," *U.S. News & World Report*, April 1, 2002.
Michelle Meadows	"Prescription Drug Use and Abuse," *FDA Consumer*, September 2001.
Eric Metcalf	"A Web of Addictions: Internet Obsessions Could Hurt Your Loved Ones Financially, Emotionally, and Physically," *Better Homes and Gardens*, May 2003.
Norbert R. Myslinkski	"Addiction's Ugly Face," *World & I*, December 1999.
National Gambling Impact Study Commission	"The Gambling Debate," *Christian Social Action*, September 1999.
Ronald M. Pavalko	"Problem Gambling," *Phi Kappa Phi Journal*, Fall 1999.
Monica Preboth	"NIAA Report on Prevention of College Drinking," *American Family Physician*, June 15, 2002.

Robert R. Selle   "Alcoholism's Nemesism," *World & I*, June
                         2000.

Mary Sojourner   "Squandering Our Kids' Inheritance," *High
                         Country News*, January 18, 1999.

S. Alex Stalcup   "High-Intensity Drugs," *Professional Counselor*,
                         February 1999.

Patricia D. Sweeting   "Gambling: The Secret Invisible Addiction,"
and Joan L. Weinberg   *Counselor*, December 2000.

What Factors Contribute to Addiction?

Chapter Preface

The relationship between teen alcohol use and adult alcohol addiction is subject to heated debate. Some analysts claim that there is a direct correlation between teen alcohol use and adult alcoholism; thus they suggest that teen alcohol policies should emphasize abstinence. Others maintain that alcohol addiction is the result of multiple factors, not just teenage drinking. They claim that teen alcohol use is a normal part of adolescent culture and disagree with abstinence policies.

A 1998 study conducted by Bridget F. Grant and Deborah A. Dawson of the National Institute on Alcohol Abuse and Alcoholism (NIAAA) revealed that young people who begin drinking before age fifteen are four times more likely to become addicted to alcohol as adults. Organizations and activists nationwide began to use such statistics to promote abstinence. A good example is prevention specialist Kay Provine, of the Hazeldon Foundation, a nonprofit organization that provides rehabilitation, education, and prevention services in the field of chemical dependency. "As soon as the study came out," says Provine, "I made a bar graph to show the correlation between early drinking and alcoholism." According to Provine, "It is so effective for parents to see something this concrete. Every year you can delay kids from using alcohol, you are buying them time."

Other commentators, even those from NIAAA, question whether the NIAAA study constitutes concrete evidence that teen alcohol use leads to adult alcoholism. When the NIAAA report was released, NIAAA director Enoch Gordis was careful to note, "We don't know what causes this extraordinary association between early drinking and later alcohol dependence." Moreover, in a June 2000 report, the same authors, Grant and Dawson, concluded, "A complex set of factors introduces individuals to alcohol and produces variations in alcohol use and abuse over the life course. Factors include psychosocial and neurobiological mechanisms as well as influences from the larger society."

Addiction author Stanton Peele, who opposes abstinence messages, points to research that draws a different conclusion about the relationship between teen alcohol use and later alcoholism. Research conducted by Harvard psychiatrist George Vaillant found that children in cultures that teach responsible drinking are less likely to develop problems with alcohol as adults than in cultures that emphasize complete abstinence. According to Peele,

> Ironically, in the United States today, we follow the method of alcohol education found least successful in the Vaillant study. That is, alcohol is grouped with illicit drugs, and children are taught that abstinence is the only answer. Yet children are aware that most adults drink, and many drink alcohol themselves on the sly. Moreover, drinking will be legal and widely available to them within a few short years. Clearly, many young people find the abstinence message confusing and hypocritical.

Commentators such as Peele who oppose teaching abstinence contend that drinking is an inevitable part of adolescent development. According to professor Rutger Engels, "Occasional drinking may be a manifestation of developmentally appropriate experimentation." In fact, Engels asserts, most teens in Western societies drink, which implies that "drinking is not only a socially acceptable behavior but also normative. Youngsters who do not drink are exceptional." Since most teens have experimented with alcohol, Engels reasons, they are likely to have had positives experiences that contradict the antidrinking messages. Engels concludes, "Therefore, health education that aims to discourage adolescents from drinking will have limited effects."

Whether or not teen alcohol use leads to alcohol addiction remains controversial. The authors of the viewpoints in the following chapter express their opinions on the factors that contribute to addiction.

"The majority of the biomedical community now considers addiction, in its essence, to be a brain disease."

Addiction Is a Brain Disease

Alan I. Leshner

Addiction is a biobehavioral disorder—a brain disease that leads to compulsive behaviors that in turn have negative health consequences for the addict, asserts Alan I. Leshner in the following viewpoint. Although addicts first voluntarily choose to use drugs, claims Leshner, research shows that their brains become altered by drug use, and most are unable to stop without medical help. Unfortunately, he argues, old ideas about the nature of addiction—that addicts are simply too weak willed to quit—keep people from seeing addiction as a chronic illness much like other brain diseases such as Alzheimer's that affect behavior. Leshner is director of the National Institute on Drug Abuse at the National Institutes of Health.

As you read, consider the following questions:
1. In Leshner's opinion, why are physical withdrawal symptoms not that important from both clinical and policy perspectives?
2. In addition to addiction, what other diseases are influenced by voluntary behavior patterns, in the author's view?
3. According to Leshner, what is one major reason why efforts to prevent drug use are so vital to the nation's drug strategy?

Alan I. Leshner, "Addiction Is a Brain Disease," *Issues in Science and Technology*, vol. 17, Spring 2001, pp. 75–80. Copyright © 2001 by *Issues in Science and Technology*. Reproduced by permission of University of Texas at Dallas, Richardson, TX.

The United States is stuck in its drug abuse metaphors and in polarized arguments about them. Everyone has an opinion. One side insists that we must control supply, the other that we must reduce demand. People see addiction as either a disease or as a failure of will. None of this bumper-sticker analysis moves us forward. The truth is that we will make progress in dealing with drug issues only when our national discourse and our strategies are as complex and comprehensive as the problem itself.

A core concept that has been evolving with scientific advances over the past decade is that drug addiction is a brain disease that develops over time as a result of the initially voluntary behavior of using drugs. The consequence is virtually uncontrollable compulsive drug craving, seeking, and use that interferes with, if not destroys, an individual's functioning in the family and in society. This medical condition demands formal treatment.

Changes in the Brain

We now know in great detail the brain mechanisms through which drugs acutely modify mood, memory, perception, and emotional states. Using drugs repeatedly over time changes brain structure and function in fundamental and long-lasting ways that can persist long after the individual stops using them. Addiction comes about through an array of neuroadaptive changes and the laying down and strengthening of new memory connections in various circuits in the brain. We do not yet know all the relevant mechanisms, but the evidence suggests that those long-lasting brain changes are responsible for the distortions of cognitive and emotional functioning that characterize addicts, particularly including the compulsion to use drugs that is the essence of addiction. It is as if drugs have highjacked the brain's natural motivational control circuits, resulting in drug use becoming the sole, or at least the top, motivational priority for the individual. Thus, the majority of the biomedical community now considers addiction, in its essence, to be a brain disease: a condition caused by persistent changes in brain structure and function.

This brain-based view of addiction has generated substantial controversy, particularly among people who seem able to think only in polarized ways. Many people erroneously still believe that biological and behavioral explanations are alternative or competing ways to understand phenomena, when in fact they are complementary and integratable. Modern science has taught that it is much too simplistic to set biology in opposition to behavior or to pit willpower against brain chemistry. Addiction involves inseparable biological and behavioral components. It is the quintessential biobehavioral disorder.

Many people also erroneously still believe that drug addiction is simply a failure of will or of strength of character. Research contradicts that position. However, the recognition that addiction is a brain disease does not mean that the addict is simply a hapless victim. Addiction begins with the voluntary behavior of using drugs, and addicts must participate in and take some significant responsibility for their recovery. Thus, having this brain disease does not absolve the addict of responsibility for his or her behavior, but it does explain why an addict cannot simply stop using drugs by sheer force of will alone. It also dictates a much more sophisticated approach to dealing with the array of problems surrounding drug abuse and addiction in our society.

The Essence of Addiction

The entire concept of addiction has suffered greatly from imprecision and misconception. In fact, if it were possible, it would be best to start all over with some new, more neutral term. The confusion comes about in part because of a now archaic distinction between whether specific drugs are "physically" or "psychologically" addicting. The distinction historically revolved around whether or not dramatic physical withdrawal symptoms occur when an individual stops taking a drug: what we in the field now call "physical dependence."

However, 20 years of scientific research has taught that focusing on this physical versus psychological distinction is off the mark and a distraction from the real issues. From both clinical and policy perspectives, it actually does not matter very much what physical withdrawal symptoms occur. Physical dependence is not that important, because even the dramatic withdrawal symptoms of heroin and alcohol addiction can now be easily managed with appropriate medications. Even more important, many of the most dangerous and addicting drugs, including methamphetamine and crack cocaine, do not produce very severe physical dependence symptoms upon withdrawal.

The Need for a Medical Model

Whether addiction is a disease or merely a choice, the utility of the medical model is needed to address resultant risks to public and individual health. A careful review of this growing body of scientific literature should offer hope that real solutions are possible. All other models for addressing drug dependence have, to date, proven to be costly failures, and doctors are not going to ignore viable treatment options for healing those suffering with drug dependence. Defining addiction as a choice only abdicates our responsibility for seeking health and true healing for our patients and, instead, leaves crushed lives dehumanized by a chronic relapsing condition with no hope for cure. As every doctor knows, "Remember to do some good" should quickly follow the first rule to "do no harm."

John H. Halpern, *Psychiatric Times*, October 2002.

What really matters most is whether or not a drug causes what we now know to be the essence of addiction: uncontrollable, compulsive drug craving, seeking, and use, even in the face of negative health and social consequences. This is the crux of how the Institute of Medicine, the American Psychiatric Association, and the American Medical Association define addiction and how we all should use the term. It is really only this compulsive quality of addiction that matters in the long run to the addict and to his or her family and that should matter to society as a whole. Compulsive craving that overwhelms all other motivations is the root cause of the massive health and social problems associated with drug addiction. In updating our national discourse on drug abuse, we should keep in mind this simple definition: Addiction is a brain disease expressed in the form of compulsive behavior. Both developing and recovering from it depend on biology, behavior, and social context.

It is also important to correct the common misimpression

that drug use, abuse, and addiction are points on a single continuum along which one slides back and forth over time, moving from user to addict, then back to occasional user, then back to addict. Clinical observation and more formal research studies support the view that, once addicted, the individual has moved into a different state of being. It is as if a threshold has been crossed. Very few people appear able to successfully return to occasional use after having been truly addicted. Unfortunately, we do not yet have a clear biological or behavioral marker of that transition from voluntary drug use to addiction. However, a body of scientific evidence is rapidly developing that points to an array of cellular and molecular changes in specific brain circuits. Moreover, many of these brain changes are common to all chemical addictions, and some also are typical of other compulsive behaviors such as pathological overeating.

Addiction should be understood as a chronic recurring illness. Although some addicts do gain full control over their drug use after a single treatment episode, many have relapses. Repeated treatments becoming necessary to increase the intervals between and diminish the intensity of relapses, until the individual achieves abstinence.

A Similarity to Other Brain Diseases

The complexity of this brain disease is not atypical, because virtually no brain diseases are simply biological in nature and expression. All, including stroke, Alzheimer's disease, schizophrenia, and clinical depression, include some behavioral and social aspects. What may make addiction seem unique among brain diseases, however, is that it does begin with a clearly voluntary behavior—the initial decision to use drugs. Moreover, not everyone who ever uses drugs goes on to become addicted. Individuals differ substantially in how easily and quickly they become addicted and in their preferences for particular substances. Consistent with the biobehavioral nature of addiction, these individual differences result front a combination of environmental and biological, particularly genetic, factors. In fact, estimates are that between 50 and 70 percent of the variability in susceptibility to becoming addicted can be accounted for by genetic factors.

Over time the addict loses substantial control over his or her initially voluntary behavior, and it becomes compulsive. For many people these behaviors are truly uncontrollable, just like the behavioral expression of any other brain disease. Schizophrenics cannot control their hallucinations and delusions. Parkinson's patients cannot control their trembling. Clinically depressed patients cannot voluntarily control their moods. Thus, once one is addicted, the characteristics of the illness—and the treatment approaches—are not that different from most other brain diseases. No matter how one develops an illness, once one has it, one is in the diseased state and needs treatment.

Moreover, voluntary behavior patterns are, of course, involved in the etiology and progression of many other illnesses, albeit not all brain diseases. Examples abound, including hypertension, arteriosclerosis and other cardiovascular diseases, diabetes, and forms of cancer in which the onset is heavily influenced by the individual's eating, exercise, smoking, and other behaviors.

The Environmental Cues

Addictive behaviors do have special characteristics related to the social contexts in which they originate. All of the environmental cues surrounding initial drug use and development of the addiction actually become "conditioned" to that drug use and are thus critical to the development and expression of addiction. Environmental cues are paired in time with an individual's initial drug use experiences and, through classical conditioning, take on conditioned stimulus properties. When those cues are present at a later time, they elicit anticipation of a drug experience and thus generate tremendous drug craving. Cue-induced craving is one of the most frequent causes of drug use relapses, even after long periods of abstinence, independently of whether drugs are available.

The salience of environmental or contextual cues helps explain why reentry to one's community can be so difficult for addicts leaving the controlled environments of treatment or correctional settings and why aftercare is so essential to successful recovery. The person who became addicted in the home environment is constantly exposed to the cues conditioned to his or her initial drug use, such as the neighborhood where he or she hung out, drug-using buddies, or the lamppost where he or she bought drugs. Simple exposure to those cues automatically triggers craving and can lead rapidly to relapses. This is one reason why someone who apparently overcame drug cravings while in prison or residential treatment could quickly revert to drug use upon returning home. In fact, one of the major goals of drug addiction treatment is to teach addicts how to deal with the cravings caused by inevitable exposure to these conditioned cues.

The Implications of Addiction as a Disease

Understanding addiction as a brain disease has broad and significant implications for the public perception of addicts and their families, for addiction treatment practice, and for some aspects of public policy. On the other hand, this biomedical view of addiction does not speak directly to and is unlikely to bear significantly on many other issues, including specific strategies for controlling the supply of drugs and whether initial drug use should be legal or not. Moreover, the brain disease model of addiction does not address the question of whether specific drugs of abuse can also be potential medicines. Examples abound of drugs that can be both highly addicting and extremely effective medicines. The best-known example is the appropriate use of morphine as a treatment for pain. Nevertheless, a number of practical lessons can be drawn from the scientific understanding of addiction.

It is no wonder addicts cannot simply quit on their own. They have an illness that requires biomedical treatment. People often assume that because addiction begins with a voluntary behavior and is expressed in the form of excess behavior, people should just be able to quit by force of will alone. However, it is essential to understand when dealing with addicts that we are dealing with individuals whose brains have been altered by drug use. They need drug addiction treatment. We know that, contrary to common belief, very few addicts actually do just stop on their own. Observing that there are very few heroin addicts in their 50s or 60s, people frequently ask what happened to those who were heroin addicts 30 years ago, assuming that they must have quit on their own. However, longitudinal studies find that only a very small fraction actually quit on their own. The rest have either been successfully treated, are currently in maintenance treatment, or (for about half) are dead. Consider the example of smoking cigarettes: Various studies have found that between 3 and 7 percent of people who try to quit on their own each year actually succeed. Science has at last convinced the public that depression is not just a lot of sadness; that depressed individuals are in a different brain state and thus require treatment to get their symptoms under control. The same is true for schizophrenic patients. It is lime to recognize that this is also the case for addicts.

Accepting Personal Responsibility

The role of personal responsibility is undiminished but clarified. Does having a brain disease mean that people who are addicted no longer have any responsibility for their behavior or that they are simply victims of their own genetics and brain chemistry? Of course not. Addiction begins with the voluntary behavior of drug use, and although genetic characteristics may predispose individuals to be more or less susceptible to becoming addicted, genes do not doom one to become an addict. This is one major reason why efforts to prevent drug use are so vital to any comprehensive strategy to deal with the nation's drug problems. Initial drug use is a voluntary, and therefore preventable, behavior.

Moreover, as with any illness, behavior becomes a critical part of recovery. At a minimum, one must comply with the treatment regimen, which is harder than it sounds. Treatment compliance is the biggest cause of relapses for all chronic illnesses, including asthma, diabetes, hypertension, and addiction. Moreover, treatment compliance rates are no worse for addiction than for these other illnesses, ranging from 30 to 50 percent. Thus, for drug addiction as well as for other chronic diseases, the individual's motivation and behavior are clearly important parts of success in treatment and recovery.

"The contention that addiction is a disease is empirically unsupported."

Addiction Is Not a Disease

Jeffrey A. Schaler

In the following viewpoint Jeffrey A. Schaler argues that addiction is a behavior, not a disease. He asserts that people voluntarily choose to consume drugs and alcohol, despite the health and social consequences. Evidence that drug use has both physical and behavioral effects, he maintains, does not mean that the physical effects of drug use cause the behavioral effect—addiction. Moreover, claims Schaler, the fact that faith-based programs such as Alcoholics Anonymous are the best treatment for addiction supports the conclusion that addiction is an ethical problem, not a disease. Schaler, professor at Johns Hopkins University in Baltimore, Maryland, is author of *Addiction Is a Choice*.

As you read, consider the following questions:

1. What are some of the ways addicts monitor their rate of drug consumption, in Schaler's opinion?
2. What did P.A. Garris, M. Kilpatrick, and M.A. Bunin discover actually triggered dopamine release as a result of their research on dopamine and the reward process in mice?
3. According to Schaler, what is the potential harm of psychotherapy as a treatment for addiction?

Jeffrey A. Schaler, "Addiction Is a Choice," *Psychiatric Times*, vol. 19, October 2002. Copyright © 2002 by CMP Media LLC. Reproduced by permission.

Is addiction a disease, or is it a choice? To think clearly about this question, we need to make a sharp distinction between an activity and its results. Many activities that are not themselves diseases can cause diseases. And a foolish, self-destructive activity is not necessarily a disease.

With those two vital points in mind, we observe a person ingesting some substance: alcohol, nicotine, cocaine or heroin. We have to decide, not whether this pattern of consumption causes disease nor whether it is foolish and self-destructive, but rather whether it is something altogether distinct and separate: Is this pattern of drug consumption itself a disease?

Addiction Is a Behavior

Scientifically, the contention that addiction is a disease is empirically unsupported. Addiction is a behavior and thus clearly intended by the individual person. What is obvious to common sense has been corroborated by pertinent research for years.

The person we call an addict always monitors their rate of consumption in relation to relevant circumstances. For example, even in the most desperate, chronic cases, alcoholics never drink all the alcohol they can. They plan ahead, carefully nursing themselves back from the last drinking binge while deliberately preparing for the next one. This is not to say that their conduct is wise, simply that they are in control of what they are doing. Not only is there no evidence that they cannot moderate their drinking, there is clear evidence that they do so, rationally responding to incentives devised by hospital researchers. Again, the evidence supporting this assertion has been known in the scientific community for years.

My book *Addiction Is a Choice* was criticized in a recent review in a British scholarly journal of addiction studies because it states the obvious. According to the reviewer, everyone in the addiction field now knows that addiction is a choice and not a disease, and I am, therefore, "violently pushing against a door which was opened decades ago." I'm delighted to hear that addiction specialists in Britain are so enlightened and that there is no need for me to argue my case over there.

In the United States, we have not made so much progress. Why do some persist, in the face of all reason and all evidence, in pushing the disease model as the best explanation for addiction?

The Relationship Between Mind and Body

I conjecture that the answer lies in a fashionable conception of the relation between mind and body. There are several competing philosophical theories about that relation. Let us accept, for the sake of argument, the most extreme "materialist" theory: the psychophysical identity theory. Accordingly, every mental event corresponds to a physical event, because it is a physical event. The relation between mind and the relevant parts of the body is, therefore, like the relation between heat and molecular motion: They are precisely the same thing, observed in two different ways. As it happens, I find this view of the relation between mind and body very congenial.

However, I think it is often accompanied by a serious misunderstanding: the notion that when we find a parallel between physiological processes and mental or personality processes, the physiological process is what is really going on and the mental process is just a passive result of the physical process. What this overlooks is the reality of downward causation, the phenomenon in which an emergent property of a system can govern the position of elements within the system. Thus, the complex, symmetrical, six-pointed design of a snow crystal largely governs the position of each molecule of ice in that crystal.

Hence, there is no theoretical obstacle to acknowledging the fact that thoughts, desires, values and other mental phenomena can dominate bodily functions. Suppose that a man's mother dies, and he undergoes the agonizing trauma we call unbearable grief. There is no doubt that if we examine this man's bodily processes we will find many physical changes, among them changes in his blood and stomach chemistry. It would be clearly wrong to say that these bodily changes cause him to be grief-stricken. It would be less misleading to say that his being grief-stricken causes the bodily changes, but this is also not entirely accurate. His knowledge of his mother's death (interacting with his prior beliefs and values) causes his grief, and his grief has blood-sugar and gastric concomitants, among many others.

The Problem with the Brain-Disease Model

Labeling addiction a chronic and relapsing brain disease is mere propaganda. By downplaying the volitional dimension of addiction, the brain-disease model detracts from the great promise of strategies and therapies that rely on sanctions and rewards to shape self-control. And by reinforcing a dichotomy between punitive and clinical approaches to addiction, the brain-disease model devalues the enormous contribution of criminal justice to combating addiction. The fact that many, perhaps most, addicts are in control of their actions and appetites for circumscribed periods of time shows that they are not perpetually helpless victims of chronic disease. They are the instigators of their own addiction, just as they can be the agents of their own recovery.

Sally L. Satel, *Public Interest*, Winter 1999.

There is no dispute that various substances cause physiological changes in the bodies of people who ingest them. There is also no dispute, in principle, that these physiological changes may themselves change with repeated doses, nor that these changes may be correlated with subjective mental states like reward or enjoyment.

Examining the Dopamine Hypothesis

I say "in principle" because I suspect that people sometimes tend to run away with these supposed correlations. For example, changes in dopamine levels have often been hypothesized as an integral part of the reward/reinforcement process. Yet research shows that dopamine in the nucleus accumbens does not mediate primary or unconditioned food reward in animals. According to [J.D.] Salamone, the theory that drugs of abuse turn on a natural reward system is simplistic and inaccurate: "Dopamine in the nucleus accumbens plays a role in the self-administration of some drugs (i.e., stimulants), but certainly not all."

[P.A.] Garris, [M. Kilpatrick, and M.A. Bunin] reached similar conclusions: "Dopamine may therefore be a neural substrate for novelty or reward expectation rather than reward itself." They concluded:

> [T]here is no correlation between continual bar pressing during [intracranial self-stimulation] and increased dopaminergic neurotransmission in the nucleus accumbens . . . our results are consistent with evidence that the dopaminergic component is not associated with the hedonistic or 'pleasure' aspects of reward. . . . Likewise, the rewarding effects of cocaine do not require dopamine; mice lacking the gene for the dopamine transporter, a major target of cocaine, will self-administer cocaine. However, increased dopamine neurotransmission in the nucleus accumbens shell is seen when rats are transiently exposed to a new environment. The increase in extracellular dopamine quickly returns to normal levels and remains there during continued exploration of the new environment . . . dopamine release in the nucleus accumbens is related to novelty, predictability or some other aspects of the reward process, rather than to hedonism itself.

Perhaps, then, some people have been too ready to jump to conclusions about specific mechanisms. Be that as it may, chemical rewards have no power to compel—although this notion of compulsion may be a cherished part of clinicians' folklore. I am rewarded every time I eat chocolate cake, but I often eschew this reward because I feel I ought to watch my weight.

An Ethical Problem

Experience with addiction treatment must surely make us even more dubious about the theory that addiction is a disease. The most popular way of helping people manage their addictive behavior is Alcoholics Anonymous (AA) and its various 12-step offshoots. Many observers have recognized the essentially religious nature of AA. The U.S. courts are increasingly regarding AA as a religious activity. In *United States v Seeger* (1965), the U.S. Supreme Court stated that the test to be applied as to whether a belief is religious is to enquire whether that belief "occupies a place in the life of its possessor parallel to that filled by the orthodox belief in God" in religions more widely accepted in the United States. This requirement is met by members of AA and other secular programs that help people with addictive behaviors and encourage their members to turn their will and lives over to the care of a supreme being. What kind of disease is this for which the best available treatment is religion? Clinical applications are based on explanations for why the behavior occurs. An activity based on a religious belief masquerading as a clinical form of treatment tells us something about what the activity really is—an ethical, not medical, problem in living.

What passes as clinical treatment for addiction is psychotherapy, which essentially consists of various forms of conversation or rhetoric. One person, the therapist, tries to influence another person, the patient, to change their values and behavior. While the conversation called therapy can be helpful, most of the conversation that occurs in therapy based on the disease model is potentially harmful. This is because the therapist misleads the patient into believing something that is simply untrue—that addiction is a disease, and, therefore, addicts cannot control their behavior. Preaching this falsehood to patients may encourage them to abandon any attempt to take responsibility for their actions.

The treatment of drug effects, at the patient's request, is well within the domain of medicine; what passes as evidence for the theory that addiction is a disease is merely clinical folklore.

> "*Marijuana is a 'gateway' drug that has enabled millions of Americans to proceed toward a miserable lifetime of drug addiction.*"

Marijuana Is a Gateway to Other Addictive Drugs

Kenneth M. Sunamoto

Marijuana use leads to the use of other illicit drugs, claims Kenneth M. Sunamoto in the following viewpoint. According to Sunamoto, the use of marijuana and other illicit drugs such as heroin and cocaine are connected because they all act on brain areas that produce dopamine—a neurotransmitter that enables people to feel good. Moreover, marijuana itself has many adverse effects on users, including physical dependence and the loss of short-term memory and psychomotor control. Sunamoto is a family physician with a special interest in addiction treatment.

As you read, consider the following questions:

1. What did Sunamoto and his staff discover from a review of the histories of severe addicts that they were trying to help?
2. In the author's opinion, in what ways does abstinence from marijuana resemble getting off heroin?
3. According to Sunamoto, what evidence shows that the genetic changes that occur as a result of marijuana use are transferred to subsequent generations?

Kenneth M. Sunamoto, "Marijuana Is Not a Safe Drug," *Honolulu Star-Bulletin*, April 21, 2000. Copyright © 2000 by *Honolulu Star-Bulletin*. Reproduced by permission of the author.

I am appalled by many of the comments being made about marijuana, within the context of legalizing medical marijuana. Yet I do not recall any inclusion of the scientific evidence that is accumulating as to the detrimental effects of marijuana.

I have personally worked for many years in the substance abuse field. On a daily basis, I see hardcore drug addicts desperately trying to recover from their severe addictions, mostly to heroin. It has destroyed their lives.

The staff and I make monumental efforts to help these individuals, with the discussion often based on "how to get them to stop." And when we review their histories, their substance abuse often includes the use of alcohol, tobacco and marijuana in their early years.

Marijuana, in fact, often has been characterized as the "gateway" drug that leads to further illicit drug use and addictions like heroin.

Examining the Evidence

In fact, sociological studies in high schools have shown that teens who use tobacco and alcohol have a 200 times greater likelihood of going on to illicit drugs such as heroin.

New scientific evidence is very clear that marijuana acts on the Mu opiate receptor sites, the same area of the brain stimulated by morphine. Heroin, after it is injected intravenously, is broken down into morphine, which stimulates the opiate receptor sites of the brain, resulting in the "high" that heroin addicts achieve.

Furthermore, it has been scientifically proven that opiates like heroin stimulants—such as cocaine, alcohol and nicotine—all act on the same area of the brain producing dopamine. Dopamine is the neurotransmitter that enables us to feel good, and is increased by marijuana.

Marijuana, unfortunately, often is characterized as being a "safe" drug. Yet its potency has grown tremendously with the selective breeding techniques boosting the active ingredient, delta-90-tetrahydrocannabinol.

The resulting physical dependence developed from chronic marijuana use will cause a much more severe abstinence syndrome when marijuana use ceases. Abstinence from marijuana may duplicate the classic "cold turkey" syndrome of getting off heroin, with symptoms including insomnia, nausea, agitation, irritability, depression and tremor.

The adverse effect of marijuana causing major havoc in our schools is its effect on learning. Short-term memory loss can be severe. The ability to learn is often impaired.

Sybrick. © 1997 by *Funny Times*. Reproduced by permission.

Recent research on the detrimental effects of drugs has been focusing more on the genetic effects of marijuana. Most studies have been concerned with the effects of illicit drug use by a pregnant mother on her unborn child.

Only a few studies have been conducted on prospective fathers. One of the most interesting involves mice exposed to marijuana.

A radioactive-isotope was attached to the marijuana, which was inhaled by the mice. This isotope could be clearly visualized with specialized instruments on the head of the sperm. It was noted that the sperm of the mice had a significant increase in the incidence of "two-headed" sperm.

The sons of these mice had a significant increase in the incidence of "two-headed" sperm as well.

This is evidence that genetic changes occur as a result of marijuana use and are genetically transferred to subsequent generations.

The effect of marijuana on psychomotor tasks is enormous. Motor vehicle accidents are prevalent when drivers are intoxicated by marijuana. The effect of recreational use of marijuana has been characterized as equivalent to .07–.10 percent blood alcohol levels. These levels are consistent with a DUI conviction in many states.

As a member of the American Society of Addiction Medicine, I have attended meetings with thousands of physicians nationwide dedicated to the fight against drug addiction. We are united in fighting the disease of drug addiction, which is so prevalent in society.

We have debated the use of marijuana in the population of outpatient addiction centers that most of us were involved in. The vast majority of the physicians felt that marijuana greatly prevented the recovery of many addicts from drug addiction.

Marijuana is a "gateway" drug that has enabled millions of Americans to proceed toward a miserable lifetime of drug addiction and suffer many severe health consequences. It is not harmless.

"Most people who try marijuana do not use it regularly and never try hard drugs."

Marijuana Is Not a Gateway to Other Addictive Drugs

Mitch Earleywine

In the following viewpoint Mitch Earleywine contends that most people who try marijuana never use hard drugs. Moreover, evidence shows that some who use hard drugs such as heroin did not use marijuana first, which means marijuana could not have caused them to use these drugs, he concludes. Lying to America's youth about marijuana leads them to question other information about the dangers of drugs and risks to their health and well being, he argues, even if that information is true. Earleywine, a professor of psychology at the University of Southern California, is author of *Understanding Marijuana*.

As you read, consider the following questions:
1. According to Earleywine, how many Americans who try marijuana never touch heroin?
2. According to the author, what determines the first drug users will select?
3. What substances do some teens choose to use if they believe that marijuana leads to hard drugs, in Earleywine's opinion?

Mitch Earleywine, "Gateway Beliefs Wreck Drug Abuse Prevention," *Drug Policy Alliance*, April 23, 2003. Copyright © 2003 by *Drug Policy Alliance*. Reproduced by permission.

Gateway theory suggests that marijuana is the first step toward painful drug addiction. Many fans of the theory think that marijuana creates an urge for hard drugs the way eating salt makes people thirsty. Two facts prove that the gateway theory is patently false. Perpetuating this lie is also incredibly dangerous.

Most Marijuana Users Do Not Touch Hard Drugs

We all may know heroin addicts who smoked marijuana, which may lead us to think that marijuana and heroin go together. But we forget the 83 million Americans who tried marijuana and never touched heroin. The chances of regularly using hard drugs after trying marijuana are small. In fact the chances of regularly using marijuana are small.

Data from the 2001 National Household Survey on Drug abuse show that if you've ever tried marijuana in your life, your chance of using other drugs in the last month is:

1 in 7 for marijuana

1 in 12 for any other illicit drug

1 in 50 for cocaine

1 in 208 for crack

1 in 677 for heroin

You're more likely to flip a coin nine times and get all 'heads' than become a regular user of heroin after trying marijuana.

In short, most people who try marijuana do not use it regularly and never try hard drugs.

Again, we all may know heroin addicts who used marijuana first. Nevertheless, research shows plenty of people, especially those with drug problems, use hard drugs before marijuana. One study showed that 39% of drug abusers started with a drug other than marijuana.

Users tend to start with whatever drug is most available. In neighborhoods filled with crack dealers, people could start with crack. But crack is not the gateway to marijuana use. Allen Ginsberg, the legendary 'Beat' poet, used heroin before marijuana. But heroin is not the gateway, either. Obviously, if marijuana use doesn't happen first, it can't cause hard drug use.

Even if every heroin addict used marijuana first, that fact

alone would not prove that marijuana caused heroin addiction. They all ate bread before their heroin addiction, but nobody has called bread the gateway drug. (At least not yet.) Marijuana doesn't cause hard drug use. People may wonder, "What's the harm in scaring teens with this little white lie, especially if it keeps them away from drugs?" Like all lies, this one catches up later. Teens who believe that marijuana leads to hard drugs end up using substances with markedly worse effects. I've had clients and students explain: "We heard pot led to heroin, so we just sniffed glue." Inhalants cause more problems than marijuana ever will, including brain damage and death.

The Common-Factor Model

Another explanation [for the link between marijuana and hard-drug use] has been suggested: Those who use drugs may have an underlying propensity to do so that is not specific to any one drug. There is some support for such a "common-factor" model in studies of genetic, familial, and environmental factors influencing drug use. The presence of a common propensity could explain why people who use one drug are so much more likely to use another than are people who do not use the first drug. It has also been suggested that marijuana use precedes hard-drug use simply because opportunities to use marijuana come earlier in life than opportunities to use hard drugs. The DPRC [Drug Policy Research Center] analysis offers the first quantitative evidence that these observations can, without resort to a gateway effect, explain the strong observed associations between marijuana and hard-drug initiation.

Drug Policy Research Center, 2002.

In addition, the gateway lie leads to hard drugs in unexpected ways. When kids try marijuana, they realize that the propaganda they've heard is untrue. They don't shoot their friends with handguns, wake up pregnant, or support terrorism. They soon suspect that other drug information is false. The teachers who said that marijuana leads to hard drugs were wrong. Why believe it when they say that crack is addictive?

The gateway lie costs us our credibility. Marijuana does not lead teens to hard drugs, but lying to them about it does.

"We might find the root cause of addiction in our genetic makeup."

Genetic Factors Contribute to Addiction

Ernest P. Noble

Some people may have a genetic predisposition to drug addiction, argues Ernest P. Noble in the following viewpoint. Noble claims that people with a gene variant, which researchers have nicknamed the "pleasure-seeking" gene, may turn to drugs to increase their levels of dopamine—a neurotransmitter that enables people to feel good. Understanding the nature of this gene, Noble contends, can lead to more effective treatment options. Noble is a professor of psychiatry and director of the Alcohol Research Center at the University of California, Los Angeles, Neuropsychiatric Institute and Hospital.

As you read, consider the following questions:
1. How did people view addiction through most of the twentieth century, in Noble's opinion?
2. In the author's view, what did research show was different about the brain tissue of those with the "pleasure-seeking" gene compared to the brain tissue of those without it?
3. According to Noble, how can addicts with a genetic predisposition to drug addiction be differentiated from those who simply developed a bad habit?

Ernest P. Noble, "Addictions May Be in the Genes," *Los Angeles Times*, December 4, 2000. Copyright © 2000 by the *Los Angeles Times*. Reproduced by permission.

Why would a talented and successful actor like Robert Downey Jr. repeatedly risk his career for the sake of a drug-induced high?

For many addicts like Downey, the answer may lie not in their upbringing or the company they keep, but in their genetic makeup.

And for drug users whose DNA plays a role in their habit, clinicians need to turn their attention to new treatment options that address the genetics of addiction.

Downey's very public yet personal struggle is a familiar story to millions of Americans who struggle with addiction. A quarter of the U.S. adult population is hooked on alcohol, cocaine, nicotine, amphetamines or some other substance.

Through most of the 20th century, we viewed addiction largely as the product of a flawed upbringing or bad character. Addicts deserved punishment, not sympathy.

The "Pleasure-Seeking" Gene

Studies comparing the lifestyles and habits of twins and adopted children first suggested that addictive behavior has a hereditary component. We began to consider the possibility that we might find the root cause of addiction in our genetic makeup. A major breakthrough in understanding the genetics of addiction came in 1990, when researchers first linked a gene called DRD2—later nicknamed the "pleasure-seeking" gene—to severe alcoholism.

UCLA [University of California at Los Angeles] studies of brain tissue showed that individuals with the "A1 variation" of the DRD2 gene have significantly fewer dopamine receptors in pleasure centers of the brain.

The findings suggest that many addicts use drugs, which increase brain dopamine levels, to compensate for the deficiency in their neurological pleasure system.

Subsequent studies linked the A1 variation of the DRD2 gene to cocaine, amphetamine, heroin and nicotine addiction.

What does this all mean? It means simply that people with this genetic trait are much more susceptible to addiction. In addition, they are more likely to fall prey to the most severe forms of addiction. In fact, data show that while only 10% of the general population in the United States has the

A1 variation of the DRD2 gene, it is found in about half of addicts.

Reexamining Treatment Options

Meanwhile, the implications for treatment programs are becoming increasingly clear. A UCLA study of heroin addicts published [in the summer of 2000] showed that a high percentage of heroin users who respond poorly to traditional addiction treatment programs have the troublesome A1 variation of the DRD2 gene.

And a recent study of alcoholics showed that patients with the same "pleasure-seeking" trait responded well to treatment with a nonaddictive drug that stimulates the dopamine receptors.

These findings demand that clinicians rethink treatment options for the millions of drug-users who are genetically predisposed to addiction.

The implications carry additional weight in California, where voter-approved Proposition 36 will divert tens of thousands of addicts a year from the criminal justice system into treatment.

Studying the Role of Genes

Why do some people become addicts while others do not? Why can some teenagers take a drink of alcohol and not crave more while others know from the instant of their first drink that alcohol is going to cause them problems for the rest of their life?

The most obvious reasons is that the susceptibility to addictive behaviors is an inborn or genetic trait. Studies of the frequency of alcoholism in children of alcoholics adopted away from their alcoholic parents at birth provide some of the most powerful evidence that our genes play an important role in the development of subsequent alcoholism.

Dr. Donald Goodman was one of the pioneers in this field. On the basis of such an adoption study he found that the frequency of alcoholism, in adopted-out sons of alcoholic fathers, was just as great when they were placed with non-alcoholic parents as with alcoholic parents. This meant that this form of alcoholism was predominantly a genetic disorder.

David E. Comings, *Addiction & Recovery*, November/December 1991.

A simple cheek cell test of DNA can help differentiate hard-core, genetic addicts from those who developed bad habits while socializing with bad crowds.

Drug abusers with a genetic propensity toward addiction typically require one of a growing number of innovative prescription drug therapies to beat their habit. Those without the gene more often respond best to counseling that addresses environmental factors that led to their drug abuse.

The more we know about why the body craves drugs and the more we put that knowledge to use, the more successful we will be in mitigating the heavy toll that drug addiction takes on individuals, families and our society.

"Addiction is a chronic, progressive, and sometimes fatal disorder with both genetic and environmental roots."

Genetic and Environmental Factors Contribute to Addiction

Judy Shepps Battle

In the following viewpoint Judy Shepps Battle claims that both genetic and environmental factors determine whether a person will develop an addiction. According to Battle, twin studies show that the children of addicts are more likely to become addicts themselves; however, environmental factors such as living in a poor, urban neighborhood also increase the likelihood that children will become addicts. One of the most important environmental factor is home life; people who come from loving, structured families are less likely to succumb to addiction, Battle maintains. Prevention programs designed to counteract environmental factors may provide potential addicts with the skills they need to escape addiction, she concludes. Battle, president of Write Action Inc., an organization devoted to helping writers promote positive social change, writes on spirituality and addiction.

As you read, consider the following questions:
1. How much money is spent annually in the United States on medical and social issues related to addiction, as cited by Battle?
2. According to Battle, what survival tools did successful adults from at-risk backgrounds use to keep from becoming addicts?

Judy Shepps Battle, "What Is Addiction?" *Psybersquare*, 2000. Copyright © 2000 by *Psybersquare*. Reproduced by permission.

Addiction is a chronic, progressive, and sometimes fatal disorder with both genetic and environmental roots. It is a compulsion that drives an individual to continue to behave in a way that is harmful to self and loved ones, despite an intense desire to halt that behavior. It is a disease of "more"—an active addict needs an increasing amount of substance to get high and is unable to cease usage without painful withdrawal symptoms. This is true whether the addictive substance is a drug—such as alcohol, tobacco, marijuana, cocaine, or heroin—or a behavior, such as gambling or sexual promiscuity.

Addiction is not confined to any economic, social, racial, religious, occupational, or age group. Addicts are not visually identifiable; it is impossible to pick out an alcoholic, drug addict, or the people who enable addictive behavior (co-dependents) from a gallery of photographs.

Alcohol, tobacco, and other drug abuse is costly. More than $275 billion dollars are spent annually in the United States on medical and social issues related to addiction. This averages out to nearly $1000 per person, whether or not that person uses drugs, because these costs include related crime, loss of work time, medical expenses from health-related injuries or illnesses, property damage, and treatment.

There is no known cure for addiction. Relapse is a part of the disease and may be triggered in a variety of environmental and emotional ways. Life-long monitoring is necessary, yet with appropriate identification, treatment, and self-care, an addict can live a productive substance-free life.

We know that addiction runs in families, but how is it transmitted? Are we born with an "addiction gene" or with an "addictive personality," or are we taught addictive behavior by our family and society? This classic question of nature vs. nurture is answered with a qualified "both."

The Genetic Causes

There is evidence that heredity plays an important part in increasing the likelihood of developing active addiction to illicit drugs, alcohol, and tobacco.

Researchers have compared alcoholism rates of adoptees born to alcoholic parents with those born to nonalcoholic parents. One study found higher alcoholism rates (two to three times higher) in sons whose natural parents were alcoholics than in sons whose natural parents were nonalcoholics. If we assume that the children studied were adopted by families with equal addiction rates, we can also assume that genetic factors play a significant role. Unfortunately, these studies could not rule out the effect of environment on their subjects.

The "Self-Medicating" Hypothesis

According to psychiatrists who have studied psychodynamic causes of drug addiction, the motivation to use psychoactive substances can often be traced to critical passages early in life. Says Edward J. Khantzian, a Harvard psychiatrist and author of the "self-medicating" hypothesis of drug addiction, many substance-dependent people who make it into therapy show a profound inability to calm and soothe themselves when stressed. The ability to self-regulate mood—to maintain psychic homeostasis—is a task learned between the ages of 1 and 3, when a toddler normally internalizes such a function from caring parents. Mothers, and no doubt many fathers, of frequent drug users have been described as "relatively cold, unresponsive and underprotective." Regarding their children's accomplishments, they send a very mixed message: They're pressuring and overly interested in their children's performance, yet rarely offer them encouragement.

Eating disorders, which are considered addictions and primarily affect women, offer a clear illustration of the self-regulation mechanism gone haywire. If the inability to soothe oneself is due to a distant or rejecting parent, compulsive eating is an attempt to make up for the loss, to construct a substitute attachment to a nurturing parent, with a primitive form of self-medication—food—one of the few things (in addition to love) that can calm a distressed child.

Michael Segell, "Big Mystery: What Causes Addiction?" MSNBC.com, 2003.

Twin studies offer more convincing evidence. Monozygotic (identical) twins share an identical genetic makeup while dizygotic (fraternal) twins share, on average, only 50 percent of genetic similarities. When we look at pairs of twins who have been raised together the variable of "environment" is controlled (not a factor).

Studies of mate twins find that identical twins have 50 to 200 percent greater rates of alcoholism than fraternal twins.

The abuse of sedatives, stimulants, cocaine, and opiates also follows this pattern and is associated with genetic predisposition.

The Environmental Factors

Although both adoption and twin studies indicate that genetic factors contribute to a predisposition for addiction, they do not tell the entire story. Environmental factors can increase the risk for developing addiction or assist in the development of resiliency skills that protect an individual from beginning to use addictive substances.

Many professionals focus primarily on environmental risk factors as determinants of a child's vulnerability to substance use and other behavioral health problems. These include demographics (geography, economics, crime rate, quality of schools) and familial factors (genetics, family addiction, family parenting skills).

A child from an urban, poor neighborhood with a high crime rate and poor school system is more likely to begin substance use than his demographic opposite. Having a family history of addiction, living with active addicts, and being inadequately parented also increases the risk of using and abusing substances.

The Tools of Prevention and Treatment

But not all kids from these high-risk environments become casualties. When we study characteristics of successful adults who come from at-risk backgrounds it is found that these adults have developed certain strengths (resiliency factors) that become survival tools.

Basic resiliency factors involve self-esteem and sound decision-making skills. Many school systems have developed curricula to foster this quality, but the primary garden of resiliency is the family.

Findings consistently show that the more adolescents feel a mix of unconditional love and loving boundaries (also called "loving control" or "loving autonomy"), the less likely they are to experience substance abuse and related problems.

Most critically, the longer initiation into substance use is delayed, the less likely addiction will result.

There is a saying that we cannot choose our family but we can choose our friends. Similarly, we have little ability to change genetic inheritance but we can support school and community prevention programs that effectively delay first use of alcohol and drugs and strengthen resiliency in at-risk youth.

If we couple this prevention effort with providing adequate treatment resources for those already addicted (and their families), we will begin to create a solid foundation for an addiction-free society.

Periodical Bibliography

The following articles have been selected to supplement the diverse views presented in this chapter.

Joseph A. Califano	"It's All in the Family," *America*, January 15, 2000.
Amal Chandra	"Addiction Is a Virus from Outer Space," *Genre*, November 1999.
Michael D. Clark	"Choice and Responsibility in Recovery from Addiction," *Counselor*, February 1999.
Anthony Daniels	"Cold Turkey Is No Worse than Flu," *New Statesman*, April 9, 1999.
Caroline Eick	"Tapping the Core," *Counselor*, August 1998.
Michael Fitzpatrick	"Addiction Addicts," *Spiked*, March 13, 2001.
Ronald Kotulak	"Everyone Is Genetically Vulnerable to Addiction," *Seattle Times*, April 4, 1999.
Donna Markus	"Of Addiction and Accountability," *Networker*, July/August 2000.
Norbert R. Myslinkski	"Addiction and the Brain," *World & I*, November 1999.
Eric J. Nester and David Landsman	"Learning About Addiction from the Genome," *Nature*, February 15, 2001.
Kim Pittaway	"Is Addiction a Choice?" *Chatelaine*, June 2000.
Wendy Richardson	"The Link Between ADHD and Addiction," *Counselor*, April 1999.
Jeff Riggenbach	"Hooked on Addiction," *Liberty*, September 2000.
Ted Roberts	"I Never Dream of Nicotine," *Ideas on Liberty*, May 2003.
Chris Sandvick	"Recovery Is Addict's Responsibility," *Counselor*, October 1998.
Sally L. Satel	"The Fallacies of No-Fault Addiction," *Public Interest*, Winter 1999.
Marc A. Schuckit and Thomas C. Jefferson	"New Findings in the Genetics of Alcoholism," *JAMA*, May 26, 1999.
Steven Stocker	"Finding the Future Alcoholic," *Futurist*, May 2002.
Jacob Sullum	"High Road: Is Marijuana a 'Gateway'?" *Reason*, March 2003.

Jacob Sullum   "H: The Surprising Truth About Heroin and Addiction," *Reason*, June 2003.

Robert A. Wascher   "Marijuana: A Gateway Drug?" *Jewish World Review*, January 23, 2003.

Alice M. Young   "Addictive Drugs and the Brain," *National Forum*, Fall 1999.

CHAPTER 3

What Are the Most Effective Treatments for Addiction?

Chapter Preface

One of many controversies in the addiction treatment debate is whether treatment for drug addicts who have been convicted of minor, nonviolent drug-related crimes should be provided in lieu of incarceration. Public attitudes toward this issue have moved in cycles. In the 1960s and 1970s, many Americans came to see drug addiction as a medical problem, and in consequence, the public concluded that treatment for drug addiction would be more effective than punishment. However, in 1979 the National Academy of Sciences reported that few of these treatment programs had a lasting positive impact, and many addicts eventually ended up in prison. Moreover, during the 1980s and early 1990s, Americans, believing crime was on the rise, favored aggressive anticrime and antidrug polices. As a result, addiction rehabilitation programs declined, and policies such as mandatory minimum sentences, which increased the sentencing times for many drug offenses, increased. As prisons became overpopulated (with no corresponding decline in drug use), American attitudes once again began to change. In 1996 the citizens of Arizona passed a treatment in lieu of incarceration initiative, and in 2000 California followed suit. While some claim these initiatives will reduce prison overpopulation and prevent the inequitable punishment of drug addicts, others think these policies must be approached with caution.

Those who support treatment in lieu of incarceration argue that implementing these policies will alleviate prison overpopulation and inequities in the criminal justice system created by aggressive anticrime laws such as mandatory minimum sentences. In the past twenty years, the incarceration rate in U.S. prisons has increased 385 percent. According to William D. McColl and Opio Sokoni of the Drug Policy Alliance, an organization working to end the war on drugs and promote new drug policies, "Much of this growth was caused by the increase in imprisonment of drug offenders. From 1987 to 1997 the number of people entering prison . . . for drug offenses increased 11-fold." Moreover, they argue, mandatory minimum sentences have created absurd criminal justice outcomes. McColl and Sokoni assert, for example, that "some low-level, nonviolent drug defendants face more severe sentences than violent offenders convicted of rape or manslaughter."

Martin Y. Iguchi, a researcher at the RAND Drug Policy Research Center, agrees that efforts to deter drug use have overloaded the criminal justice system. He argues, however, that as a solution to this problem, treatment programs in lieu of incarceration have several drawbacks. He maintains, for example, that there are a limited number of treatment slots available at any given time, and mandatory treatment in lieu of incarceration will use up most if not all of these slots. Iguchi cautions, "We do not want someone who is voluntarily seeking treatment to be deprived of that opportunity because the slot has been filled with an individual mandated to receive treatment." Iguchi also warns that the policy could be abused if prosecutors instead of judges manage the drug courts that administer these programs. "Some public defenders and defense attorneys," he explains, "have voiced concern that prosecutors may be tempted to offer access to drug court only to those individuals who are 'cooperative.'" Such policies, he argues, use treatment as a weapon rather than a tool, which defeats the purpose of the program—to help all nonviolent drug addicts recover and stay out of prison.

Whether or not treatment in lieu of incarceration is effective continues to be fervently disputed. The authors of the viewpoints in the following chapter express their opinions on other controversial treatment options.

*"The 12-step-oriented programs were not
only cost-efficient, they were also effective."*

Twelve-Step Programs Are an Effective Treatment for Addiction

Krista Conger

In the following viewpoint Krista Conger, who represents the Office of Communications and Public Affairs for the Stanford Medical Center, claims that a study conducted by the center found that the twelve-step approach to addiction treatment is less expensive and more effective than cognitive-behavioral approaches. Twelve-step approaches (such as Alcoholics Anonymous) emphasize seeking spiritual help for substance-abuse problems, Conger maintains, while cognitive-behavioral programs teach coping skills. According to Conger, the study suggests that twelve-step treatment approaches save money because patients seek self-help rather than medical help upon release from treatment centers. Moreover, nearly 46 percent of those in twelve-step programs remained sober one year after discharge, she claims. Conger writes for *Stanford Medicine* and *Stanford Report*.

As you read, consider the following questions:

1. In Conger's view, what has happened to funding for substance abuse treatment programs nationwide in recent years?
2. How might treatment programs around the United States benefit from the study's conclusions, in Conger's opinion?

Krista Conger, "Study Points Out Value of 12-Step Groups in Treating Substance Abuse," *Stanford Report*, May 23, 2001. Copyright © 2001 by *Stanford Report*. Reproduced by permission.

Inpatient substance abuse treatment programs emphasizing the spiritually oriented "12-step" approach to addiction save money and promote abstinence more effectively than treatment programs that emphasize practical coping skills, say medical school researchers. Graduates from the 12-step-oriented programs slice their long-term health care costs by more than half by turning to community-based self-help groups rather than to professional mental health services for support in the year after discharge, say the researchers. They are also significantly more likely to remain abstinent in the year following their treatment.

"Groups like Alcoholics Anonymous and Narcotics Anonymous are taking a huge burden off of the health care system," said Keith Humphreys, PhD. "We found that addiction treatment programs are more effective and less expensive when they link patients to spiritually based self-help groups."

Humphreys, assistant professor of psychiatry and behavioral science [at Stanford University], is the lead author of the study published in the May [2001] issue of *Alcoholism: Clinical and Experimental Research*. Humphreys is also the associate director of the Program Evaluation and Resource Center at the Veterans Affairs Palo Alto Health Care System in Menlo Park, Calif.

Although one-quarter of all deaths in this country are caused by alcohol, tobacco or illegal drugs, funding for substance abuse treatment programs nationwide has decreased dramatically in recent years, Humphreys said. "Most mental health treatment professionals are being asked to do more and more with less and less," he said. He and co-author Rudolf Moos, PhD, investigated whether free, community-based support groups could stand in for professional mental health treatment, reducing health care costs without compromising patient outcome.

Comparing Treatment Programs

Humphreys studied 1,774 low-income, substance-dependent men who had been enrolled in inpatient substance abuse treatment programs at 10 Department of Veteran Affairs medical centers around the country. Five of the programs strongly emphasized the 12-step approach to addiction, a spiritually oriented philosophy that urges individuals to take responsibility for their actions and ask for help from God in conquering their dependency. These programs frequently hold Alcoholics Anonymous or Narcotics Anonymous meetings on-site, and refer to the "Big Book," an inspirational text that complements the 12 steps.

The Twelve Steps

1. We admitted we were powerless over alcohol, that our lives had become unmanageable.

2. Came to believe that a Power greater than ourselves could restore us to sanity.

3. Made a decision to turn our will and our lives over to the care of God *as we understood Him.*

4. Made a searching and fearless moral inventory of ourselves.

5. Admitted to God, to ourselves, and to another human being the exact nature of our wrongs.

6. Were entirely ready to have God remove all these defects of character.

7. Humbly asked Him to remove our shortcomings.

8. Made a list of all persons we had harmed, and became willing to make amends to them all.

9. Made direct amends to such people wherever possible, except when to do so would injure them or others.

10. Continued to take personal inventory and when we were wrong promptly admitted it.

11. Sought through prayer and meditation to improve our conscious contact with God *as we understood Him*, praying only for knowledge of His will for us and the power to carry that out.

12. Having had a spiritual awakening as the result of these steps, we tried to carry this message to alcoholics, and to practice these principles in all our affairs.

Alcoholics Anonymous, 2001.

The remaining five programs used an approach called cognitive-behavioral therapy that concentrates on teaching individuals coping skills to avoid relapse. These programs, which emphasized a medical and scientific approach to addiction treatment, spent only about 7 percent of treatment time discussing the 12-step approach. The men in the study were evenly divided between the two types of programs.

Humphreys paired up men from the two programs whose mental health care costs in the year preceding treatment were similar. He then compared the mental health care costs between the men in the year following discharge. He found that the total mental health care costs for men enrolled in cognitive-behavioral programs were about $4,700 higher than those for men enrolled in 12-step-oriented programs, even though their starting values were similar.

The cost difference was attributed to the increased likelihood of men enrolled in the 12-step-oriented approach to attend meetings of community-based self-help groups after discharge while also being less likely to seek help from traditional medical professionals to avoid relapsing.

The 12-step-oriented programs were not only cost-efficient, they were also effective—nearly 46 percent of the men in these programs were abstinent one year after discharge, compared to 36 percent of those treated in cognitive-behavioral programs. This may be due in part to strong endorsements from staff members at the 12-step-oriented programs who are more likely to be recovering addicts.

"They tend to be people who really believe in the approach they're teaching," said Humphreys. "They are more likely to say, 'I can help you overcome your cocaine addiction, because I overcame one.'" Once the patients of these programs are discharged, they can call on self-help group members and sponsors they met during their treatment, creating a mutual support network that can in some ways mirror the support provided by professional counselors.

The study suggests that it may be beneficial for treatment programs around the United States to incorporate more of the 12-step philosophy into their substance abuse therapies, and to increase their efforts to link patients with community-based self-help groups after discharge.

"In the current health care climate, a clinical strategy that reduces the ongoing health care costs of substance abuse patients by 64 percent while also promoting good outcome deserves serious attention," Humphreys and Moos concluded in the paper.

"The view that one can only recover via the moral improvement of the 12 steps is doing more harm than good."

Twelve-Step Programs Are Inadequate to Treat Addiction

Maia Szalavitz

By rejecting all alternative treatment options, twelve-step treatment programs such as Alcoholics Anonymous prevent some people from getting the help they need, argues Maia Szalavitz in the following viewpoint. These programs emphasize faith in God over scientific fact, she maintains, and thus reject empirically proven treatments for addiction. For example, Szalavitz claims, twelve-step programs reject the use of medication by alcoholics suffering from diseases such as depression despite the scientifically proven relief medication can provide. Moreover, argues Szalavitz, twelve-step programs support punitive drug policies that contradict their claim that addiction is a disease, not a sin. Szalavitz, a science journalist, is the author of *Recovery Options: The Complete Guide*.

As you read, consider the following questions:

1. According to Szalavitz, what has happened to the twelve-step movement since the 1980s and 1990s?
2. What happened during the last five years of the author's experience in a twelve-step recovery program?
3. In Szalavitz's opinion, how do twelve-step treatment providers characterize addiction to secure support from the drug-war establishment?

Maia Szalavitz, "Breaking Out of the 12-Step Lockstep," *Washington Post*, June 9, 2002, p. B03. Copyright © 2002 by Washington Post Book World Service/ Washington Post Writers Group. Reproduced by permission of the author.

In the 1980s and '90s, 12-step programs like Alcoholics Anonymous [AA] were the gold standard for addiction treatment. Even among the non-addicted, they had become an accepted part of American culture. In Tim Robbins's 1992 film, *The Player*, the title character attended AA meetings not because he drank too much but because that's where the deals were being made. In 1995, *New York* magazine suggested that single women attend AA to meet men.

But today, the recovery movement—with its emphasis on childhood victimization, lifetime attendance at 12-step groups and complete abstinence from all psychoactive substances—has fallen from pop culture favor. "There was a time when it was almost the 'in thing' to say you were in recovery," says William White, author of *Slaying the Dragon*, a history of addiction treatment. Thankfully, that is no longer the case.

Vogue, *Elle* and the *New York Times Magazine* have recently run articles critical of the recovery movement. The "addictions" section of the bookstore—once taking up several bookcases in superstores—has shrunk to a few shelves, with a growing proportion of critical books. By the late '90s, the number of inpatient rehab facilities offering treatment centered on the 12-step process was half what it had been earlier in the decade. And AA membership, which grew explosively from the late '70s through the late '80s, has held steady at about 2 million since 1995.

Examining 12-Step Contradictions

Still, it is difficult to say goodbye to an organization and philosophy that may have helped save my life. Between the ages of 17 and 23, I was addicted to cocaine and then heroin. For the next 12 years, I was an often enthusiastic participant in 12-step recovery. Eventually, however, it became difficult to imagine defining myself for the rest of my life in relation to behavior that had taken up so few years of it.

During my last five years in the program, I had become increasingly uncomfortable with what it presented as truth: the notion, for example, that addiction is a "chronic, progressive disease" that can only be arrested by 12-stepping. The more research I did, the more I learned that much of what I had been told in rehab was wrong. And yet, I'd indisputably gotten better. Once an unemployed, 80-pound wreck, I had become a healthy, productive science journalist. That science part, however, became the root of my problem with a model based on anecdote as anodyne.

The 12-step model has always been rife with contradiction. Its adherents recognize, for example, that addiction is a disease, not a sin. But their treatment isn't medical; it's praying, confession and meeting. And while they claim that the belief in a "God of your understanding" on which the program rests is spiritual, not religious, every court that has ever been asked whether ordering people into such programs violates the separation of church and state has disagreed with the "non-religious" label.

So why have the contradictions come to the fore now? For me, the first step came in 2000 when I wrote about New York's Smithers Addiction Treatment and Research Center and its attempts to modernize treatment. Its director, Alex DeLuca, saw that options needed to be expanded beyond AA. Guided by DeLuca, Smithers began publishing studies funded by the National Institute on Alcoholism and Alcohol Abuse showing that adding treatment options, including support for moderation rather than abstinence, was effective.

Protesting Evidence-Based Options

However, when a group of people in recovery learned that those options included moderation, they protested, and DeLuca was fired. Imagine cancer or AIDS patients demonstrating against evidence-based treatment offering more options. This deeply distressed me, as did AA's religious aspects. In any other area of medicine, if a physician told you the only cure for your condition was to join a support group that involves "turning your will and your life" over to God (AA's third step), you'd seek a second opinion.

The insistence on the primacy of God in curing addiction also means that treatment can't change in response to empirical evidence. Which leaves us with a rehab system based more on faith than fact. Nowhere is this clearer than in the field's response to medication use. The National Institute on Drug Abuse is pouring big bucks into developing "drugs to fight drugs" but, once approved, they sit on the shelves because many rehab facilities don't believe in medication. Until 1997, for example, the well-known rehab facility Hazelden refused to provide antidepressants to people who had both depression and addiction.

A Treatment Monopoly

The AA [Alcoholics Anonymous] 12-step industry maintains a virtual monopoly over the nation's recovery programs. Though AA 12-step programs are open to all who wish to participate, they remain surprisingly antagonistic to partnering with medical scientists—this in spite of AA cofounder Bill Wilson's recognition nearly 50 years ago that the "discoveries of the psychiatrists and biochemists have vast implications for us alcoholics."

Manijeh Nikakhtar and Louis F. Markert, *Family Practice News*, July 15, 2001.

Those who promote just one means of recovery are right to find medication threatening. When I finally tried antidepressants, after years of resisting "drugs" because I'd been told they might lead to relapse, my disillusionment with the recovery movement grew. Years of groups and talking couldn't do what those pills did: allow me not to overreact emotionally, and thus to improve my relationships and worry less. I didn't need to "pray for my character defects to be lifted" (AA's 6th and 7th steps)—I needed to fix my brain chemistry.

This is not to say that I didn't learn anything through recovery groups. The problem is their insistence that their solutions should trump all others. Many recovering people now use medication and groups both—but within the movement there is still an enormous hostility toward this and a sense that people on medications are somehow cheating by avoiding the pain that leads to emotional growth.

Questionable Motives

Another contradiction in the notion of 12-step programs as a medical treatment shows up in the judicial system. Logically, if addiction were a disease, prison and laws would have no place in its treatment. However, to secure support from the drug-war establishment, many 12-step treatment providers argue that addiction is a disease characterized by "denial"—

despite research showing that addicts are no more likely to be in denial than people with other diseases, and that most addicts tell the truth about their drug use when they won't be punished for doing so.

Because of "denial," however, many in-patient treatment providers use methods that would be unheard of for any other condition: restrictions on food and medications, limits on sleep, hours of forced confessions and public humiliation, bans on contact with relatives and, of course, threats of prison for noncompliance.

If these programs wanted what was best for their patients, they would support measures to fund more treatment and divert people from jail. Watching famous 12-steppers such as Martin Sheen fight against California's Proposition 36, which mandates treatment rather than punishment for drug possession, was the final straw for me.

If their argument is that people won't attend treatment without the threat of prison, how do they explain all the alcoholics they treat? How, for that matter, do they explain that 12-step programs were started by volunteers? Their opposition only makes sense in the context of a view of addicts as sinners, not patients.

The view that one can only recover via the moral improvement of the 12 steps is doing more harm than good. It is supporting bad drug policy, preventing people from getting the treatment they need and hampering research.

Yet it is important not to dismiss 12-step programs entirely. They provide a supportive community and should be recommended as an option for people with addictions. Let evidence-based research determine how people are treated medically for drug problems.

"God, religion and spirituality are key factors for many in prevention and treatment of substance abuse and in continuing recovery."

Spirituality Can Help Those Trying to Recover from Addiction

National Center on Addiction and Substance Abuse

People of all ages who attend religious services and who consider religious beliefs important are less likely to abuse alcohol or drugs, according to a study summarized in the following viewpoint. Conducted by the National Center on Addiction and Substance Abuse (CASA) at Columbia University in New York City, the study analyzed research from a variety of sources and concluded that spiritual faith is an important element in substance-abuse treatment. These results, CASA maintains, should encourage cooperation among the clergy, the medical community, and treatment providers to provide faith-based programs for patients struggling with addiction.

As you read, consider the following questions:

1. According to the authors of the CASA study, what percentage of clergy members recognized substance abuse as an important issue among family members in their congregations?
2. In the opinion of the authors of the CASA study, what should physicians and substance-abuse treatment specialists discuss with patients?

National Center on Addiction and Substance Abuse, *So Help Me God: Substance Abuse, Religion, and Spirituality*. New York: National Center on Addiction and Substance Abuse at Columbia University, 2001. Copyright © 2001 by the National Center on Addiction and Substance Abuse at Columbia University. Reproduced by permission.

Ninety-five percent of Americans profess a belief in God. For many individuals, religion and spirituality are important components of prevention and treatment of substance abuse and of successful recovery. One has only to listen to the voices of recovery to hear how eloquently they speak about the role of religion or spirituality in their own healing process.

A Spiritual Connection

CASA's [National Center on Addiction and Substance Abuse] research has identified an important connection between spiritual and religious practices and lower risk of substance abuse:

- CASA's annual teen surveys have consistently demonstrated that adolescents who attend religious services are less likely to report substance use.
- CASA's study, *Under the Rug: Substance Abuse and the Mature Woman* revealed that 91 percent of woman over the age of 59 who did not identify themselves as religious consumed alcohol compared with 64 percent who identified themselves as Catholic and 52 percent who identified themselves as Protestant. Similarly, mature women who say they are not religious are more likely to be current smokers (45 percent) than those who are Catholic (25 percent) or Protestant (21 percent).
- Roughly one-third of prison inmates participates in religious activities and those who do so have been found to exhibit lower rates of recidivism.
- CASA's CASASTART (Striving to Achieve Rewarding Tomorrows) parent program found that participating children had less past month drug use, delinquency and other problems, and that the most frequently attended activities were those sponsored by religious organizations.

A Source of Hope

These findings and experience have led CASA to explore . . . the link between God, religion and spirituality and substance abuse prevention, treatment and recovery, and how to better exploit any such link. By examining recent findings in practice and research with respect to the role of religion and spirituality in dealing with substance abuse and by listening to the voices of recovery, CASA aims to draw attention to a powerful source of hope for many affected by this disease.

As part of this two-year study, CASA conducted two unprecedented surveys: one, asking presidents of schools of theology and seminaries about their perceptions of the extent of substance abuse problems and the formal training and coursework offered in this subject; the other, asking clergy in the field their perspective of these problems among their congregations and what training they had received in this area.

CASA conducted its own special analyses of three national data sets: *1998 National Household Survey on Drug Abuse;* CASA's Back to School Surveys—*Back to School 1999—National Survey of American Attitudes on Substance Abuse V: Teens and Their Parents* and *National Survey of American Attitudes on Substance Abuse VI: Teens;* and the General Social Survey. CASA undertook an extensive review of more than 300 publications that examine the link between spirituality, religiousness and substance abuse and addiction. Finally, CASA looked at a wide range of programs that incorporate spiritual or religious components in their prevention or treatment programs.

Most data and research on the link between substance abuse and religion and spirituality are limited to the Protestant and Catholic religions and to a lesser extent the Jewish faith. Unfortunately, we were unable to find any significant information in Islam, Buddhism or Hinduism.

Summarizing

Key Findings

- God, religion and spirituality are key factors for many in prevention and treatment of substance abuse and in continuing recovery.
- Adults who do not consider religious beliefs important are more than one and one-half times likelier to use alcohol and cigarettes, more than three times likelier to binge drink, almost four times likelier to use an illicit drug other than marijuana and more than six times likelier to use marijuana than adults who strongly be-

lieve that religion is important.

- Adults who never attend religious services are almost twice as likely to drink, three times likelier to smoke, more than five times likelier to have used an illicit drug other than marijuana, almost seven times likelier to binge drink and almost eight times likelier to use marijuana than those who attend religious services at least weekly.
- Teens who do not consider religious beliefs important are almost three times likelier to drink, binge drink and smoke, almost four times likelier to use marijuana and seven times likelier to use illicit drugs than teens who strongly believe that religion is important.
- Teens who never attend religious services are twice as likely to drink, more than twice as likely to smoke, more than three times likelier to use marijuana and binge drink and almost four times likelier to use illicit drugs than teens who attend religious services at least weekly.
- Children who strongly believe that religion is important report learning more about the risks of drugs. When discussing drugs with their parents, 63.5 percent of teens who strongly believe religion is important feel they learned a lot about the risks of drugs; only 41 percent who believe religion is not important feel they learned a lot.
- College students with no religious affiliation report higher levels of drinking and binge drinking than those of either Catholic or Protestant religious affiliation.
- Ninety-four percent of clergy members—priests, ministers and rabbis—recognize substance abuse as an important issue among family members in their congregations and almost 38 percent believe that alcohol abuse is involved in half or more of the family problems they confront.
- Only 12.5 percent of clergy completed any coursework related to substance abuse while studying to be a member of the clergy and only 25.8 percent of presidents of schools of theology and seminaries report that individuals preparing for the ministry are required to take courses on this subject.

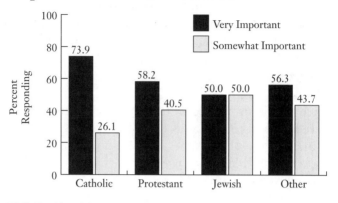

Presidents of Schools of Theology Rate Importance of Substance Abuse

Very Important
Somewhat Important

Catholic: 73.9 / 26.1
Protestant: 58.2 / 40.5
Jewish: 50.0 / 50.0
Other: 56.3 / 43.7

(Percent Responding)

CASA Presidents' Survey, 2001.

- Only 36.5 percent of clergy report that they preach a sermon on substance abuse more than once a year; 22.4 percent say they never preach on the subject.
- Seventy-nine percent of Americans believe that spiritual faith can help people recover from disease and 63 percent think that physicians should talk to patients about spiritual faith. One study found that 99 percent of family physicians are convinced that religious beliefs can heal and 75 percent believe that prayers of others can promote a patient's recovery. However, 74 percent of psychiatrists disapprove of praying with a patient; only 37 percent say they would pray with a patient even if provided with scientific evidence that doing so would improve patient progress. Only 57 percent would recommend that a patient consult with a member of the clergy.
- Individuals who attend spiritually-based support programs, such as 12-Step programs of Alcoholics Anonymous [AA] and Narcotics Anonymous [NA], in addition to receiving treatment are more likely to maintain sobriety. Individuals in successful recovery often show greater levels of faith and spirituality than individuals who relapse.

Despite these facts, spirituality and religion are often

overlooked as relevant factors in preventing and treating substance abuse and addiction.

Each religious and spiritual tradition has it own unique beliefs, commitments and rituals to bring to bear to minimize substance abuse and to aid recovery. To take advantage of the potentially positive benefits of religion and spirituality to prevent substance abuse and help individuals, CASA recommends a series of steps to combine the resources of religion and spirituality with those of science and medicine in order to enhance the prevention and treatment of substance abuse and to strengthen and maintain recovery:

The Next Step for Clergy

- Protestant, Catholic, Rabbinical and other schools of theology and seminaries should train clergy to recognize the signs and symptoms of substance abuse and know how to respond, including referral to treatment and strategies for relapse prevention. These schools should provide basic educational and clinical knowledge of the short and long term effects of tobacco, alcohol and other drugs and educate their students about ways to incorporate prevention messages both formally and informally into their work. They should educate their students about the co-occurrence of mental health and other problems (such as domestic violence and child abuse) and substance abuse. These schools should include courses related to substance abuse in degree requirements and provide in-service training for current clergy.
- Clergy members who have completed their formal training should take advantage of additional substance abuse training in order to be knowledgeable about the topic. Resources include: local public substance abuse treatment agencies, private licensed substance abuse professionals, substance abuse professional organizations such as the National Association of State Alcohol and Drug Agency Directors (NASADAD), federal resources such as the National Institute on Drug Abuse and the National Institute on Alcohol Abuse and Alcoholism, the U.S. Department of Health and Human Services Substance Abuse and Mental Health Services

Administration and its Centers for Substance Abuse Prevention and Substance Abuse Treatment.

- Members of the clergy should preach about substance abuse issues and informally include messages about the problem throughout their organization's programs, services and counseling. Even religions with assigned readings and themes for sermons can incorporate messages about substance abuse as examples and prayers for those addicted in their services. Recognizing that substance abuse affects individuals and families in all congregations, clergy can inform their members with prevention messages, and help connect members of their community to needed intervention and treatment resources and, as many presently do, open their facilities to AA and NA meetings.

- Members of the clergy should reach out to treatment programs to offer spiritual support to individuals who desire such assistance. Clergy can help educate treatment providers of the promising effects of spirituality and religion in recovery. Clergy should learn about treatment programs in their communities. By building this relationship, clergy will know who to refer members to for treatment and know how to support referrals from treatment providers of clients seeking to deepen their spiritual life.

Participants in recovery may have great needs for spiritual guidance. Individuals struggling to recover may feel abandoned by God or alienated from God or the religious community. Clergy can help recovering individuals navigate these issues and benefit from a connection to a loving God and religious community.

The Future of Treatment

For many individuals, spirituality and religiousness can be important companions to recovery and maintaining sobriety.

- Physician and other health professions training programs should educate physicians and treatment specialists to understand that many patients desire spiritual help as complements to medical treatment, and the research documenting the benefits of spirituality and religiousness to physical and mental health.

- Physicians and substance abuse treatment specialists should discuss patients' spiritual needs and desires and, where appropriate, refer clients to clergy or spiritually-based programs to support their recovery.
- Substance abuse treatment providers (physicians and other health clinicians) should establish working relationships with local clergy members not only to educate clergy members about substance abuse but also to better respond to patients needs and desires for a spiritual complement to their recovery regimen.
- More research is needed to evaluate the efficacy and increase the effectiveness of faith-based prevention initiatives and treatment programs, develop better ways of measuring adolescent spirituality and religiousness and document pathways through which religion and spirituality work to prevent substance abuse and aid in recovery.

> *"With the number of non-religious adults increasing . . . , it is imperative to find ways to reach this group with [substance-abuse] education and treatment options which they can accept."*

The Importance of Spirituality in Addiction Recovery Is Exaggerated

Kevin Courcey

According to Kevin Courcey in the following viewpoint, research claiming that religious faith helps keep Americans from abusing drugs and alcohol is flawed. He claims that such studies, which are funded by groups working to make religion more central to American society, inflate the number of religious believers, create misleading categories that distort the results, and exaggerate the severity of alcohol abuse. Despite claims by these researchers, the number of nonbelievers is growing nationwide, Courcey claims; developing nonreligious-based treatment options for those individuals will become increasingly important. Courcey is a registered nurse at Humboldt County Mental Health in Eureka, California.

As you read, consider the following questions:

1. In Courcey's opinion, why is the American Religious Identification Survey, conducted by the City University of New York, more objective than the Gallup Poll?
2. According to the author, how did the CASA study define alcohol abuse?

Kevin Courcey, "The Devil Made Me Do It," *American Atheist*, vol. 40, Winter 2001–2002, pp. 39–42. Copyright © 2002 by *American Atheist*. Reproduced by permission.

In a report published in November of 2001, Columbia University's Center on Addiction and Substance Abuse (CASA) reviewed the statistics on religiosity and substance abuse in adults and teens. They also "conducted an unprecedented survey of attitudes and experiences" of members of the clergy about their perceptions of substance abuse problems in their congregations, and their preparedness to deal with those problems. In a summary statement, CASA President Joseph Califano Jr., former head of Health, Education and Welfare under [former president] Jimmy Carter, writes:

> The key finding of this two-year study is this: if ever the sum were greater than the parts it is in combining the power of God, religion and spirituality with the power of science and professional medicine to prevent and treat substance abuse and addiction. A better understanding by the clergy of the disease of alcohol and drug abuse and addiction among members of their congregations and a better appreciation by the medical profession, especially psychiatrists and psychologists, of the power of God, religion and spirituality to help patients with this disease hold enormous potential for prevention and treatment of substance abuse and addiction that can help millions of Americans and their families.

The study emphasizes that we are a country of "believers"; that 95% of us believe in God, 92% are affiliated with an established religion, "In God We Trust" is emblazoned on our currency, *etc.* They boldly assert that non-believers are more prone to substance abuse:

> Adults who never attend religious services are almost twice as likely to drink, three times likelier to smoke, five times likelier to use illicit drugs other than marijuana, seven times likelier to binge drink and almost eight times likelier to use marijuana than adults who attend religious services weekly or more.

These are horrifying statistics. It would seem that non-believers are a bunch of low-life scum who are half in the bag most of the time on any of a half-dozen different legal and illegal drugs, while religious folks are content to go to church several times a week and spend their free time volunteering at their local homeless shelters.

But perhaps a closer look at this research is in order.

As those of you who are familiar with this genre of research might have guessed, this research was funded by the

Templeton Foundation. The Templeton Foundation's stated goat is: "By promoting collaboration and clinical research into the relationship between spirituality and health and documenting the positive medical aspects of spiritual practice, the Foundation hopes to contribute to the reintegration of faith into modern life." Notice that the Foundation is only interested in funding research that documents the positive medical effects of religion and spirituality. This puts significant pressure on the researchers to "mine the data" until they can come up with positive findings.

Singled out for his contribution to this research was David Larson, M.D., President of the International Center for the Integration of Health and Spirituality (formerly called the National Institute for Health Care Research). The Templeton Foundation funds Larson's spirituality and health research ventures at roughly $3–4 million per year. The CASA study also frequently cites Templeton-funded researchers Harold Koenig and Michael McCullough to bolster their claims for the positive effects of religion on health.

The Bodman Foundation also helped fund this research. Like the Templeton Foundation. this group also has a conservative, religious viewpoint, and is known for funding religious homeless programs, school-choice/voucher research, sexual abstinence-only programs, welfare-to-work reform, and faith-based solutions to drug abuse, teen pregnancy, and youth violence. It was at the request of the Bodman Foundation that this research was undertaken.

Evaluating the Data

CASA used several data sets to generate their figures. Much of their religious affiliation and religious belief data was obtained from surveys done by the Gallup Poll. This organization has been accused of slanting their survey questions over the years to inflate the apparent number of religious believers in the country. For example, what started out in the '50s as "Do you believe in the God of the Bible?" has devolved into questions about belief in a "universal spirit" or "animating force."

Fortunately [in 2001], the City University of New York repeated their American Religious Identification Survey (ARIS).

ARIS surveyed over 50,000 households about their religious beliefs, affiliation with specific denominations, church attendance, *etc.* Since the ARIS survey was not funded by religious organizations, its data are more objective and designed to elicit a deeper understanding of religious belief in America. In fact, ARIS specifically changed the wording of the question they used to ascertain religious identification, adding the phrase "if any" to make the question "What is your religion, if any?" They did this because they felt that previous surveys (such as those used by Gallup) had subtly influenced respondents to choose a religion by not offering an alternative. Whether as a result of this change, or reflecting a major shift away from belief in the population, they found that the number of people choosing "none" or "no religion" has more than doubled since 1990. While the ARIS survey did not investigate substance abuse, it does give us a more reliable reference paint to evaluate the claims for religious belief and participation made by the CASA study, which based its data primarily on the more limited General Social Survey, and data supplied by Gallup.

The Claims and Proposed Solutions

The CASA report can be summarized as follows:

We are a nation of believers and our faith is very important to us.

Religious faith and practice has a prophylactic effect against substance abuse.

Religious faith and practice can be essential in recovery from substance abuse.

Non-believers abuse substances at significantly higher rates.

The clergy believe substance abuse is a big problem.

The clergy is unprepared to deal with substance abuse problems.

The medical establishment, especially mental health professionals, are unreasonably reluctant to use religious interventions with clients.

The clergy therefore need to be trained on how to handle substance-abuse problems, and should preach about this topic from the pulpit.

The clergy should contact local treatment centers in order to offer their services to the clients there, and to educate the providers on the "promising effects" of religious counseling on substance-abuse treatment.

Physicians should recognize that many clients desire spiritual help, and should refer them to spiritually based treatment programs.

The report makes it obvious that in order to cut down on teen drug use, parents should impress upon our youth the importance of religion and make sure they attend religious services at least weekly. The report also stresses the need to provide religious treatment options to all clients with substance-abuse problems. It is implied that intervention strategies that do not incorporate God and religion are likely to fail.

This focus fits well with the Tempteton goal of "reintegrating" faith into our lives, and they are more than willing to impose that goal on a vulnerable population seeking treatment for addiction.

The Art of Skewing a Survey

Several methods were used to skew the results of this survey. First, the figures used for religious identification and practice were inflated. While the CASA report repeatedly states that 95% of Americans believe in God, and that 92% of us are affiliated with a specific religion, the 2001 ARIS survey shows this to be false. The percentage of American adults who self identify with a specific religion has dropped to 81%. Of those who do claim a religious affiliation, 40% stated that neither they nor their family members attend services. The ARIS survey also found that 14% of those surveyed chose "no religion." This means that a substantial majority of the adults in this country either profess no religion, or have so little interest in organized religion that neither they nor their family members go to services. This fatally undercuts the argument that the way to curb drug abuse is to train clergy. Why expend resources addressing the problem where, according to their data, it is least prevalent? This would be equivalent to saying that since syphilis is concentrated in the South, and living on the West coast seems to have a prophylactic effect against contracting syphilis, we should better educate medical professionals in the west on how to treat syphilis.

'It's a side-effect from giving up booze.'

The Spectator. © 1996 by *The Spectator*. Reproduced by permission.

Why would CASA use inflated figures for religious belief? In order to project the image of a huge, receptive client base for religiously oriented intervention services, of course. This would then be used to justify funneling taxpayer funds to these faith-based groups. But aren't they simultaneously saying that the religious are less likely to abuse substances? Yes, but for them there is no contradiction in saying that the non-religious are more likely to abuse substances so we should train the clergy to treat them. One need only recall that the goal of the Templeton Foundation is to reintegrate faith into American life. This approach is not as concerned with appropriately treating an illness as it is with bringing the wayward sheep back into the fold.

Their approach is likely doomed to failure, in any case. When Templeton funded Dale Matthews to do research evaluating Christian prayer for arthritis sufferers in conservative Florida, they were unable to recruit sufficient volunteers to carry out their research design. A public demand for religiously oriented healthcare interventions is not going to materialize just because Templeton and CASA would like it to happen.

Using Arbitrary Definitions

The second method used to skew this survey was arbitrarily defining the groups to be studied. If one's goal were to show the religious to be a relatively healthy norm, while non-believers are shown to be a drug-abusing fringe group, you would need to artificially expand the religious group and restrict the non-believer group to achieve this end.

In order to expand the "religious" category, the concept of being "spiritual" was added to it. This is how the CASA group defined spirituality for the purposes of this report:

> Spirituality, on the other hand, is a deeply personal and individualized response to God, a higher power or an animating force in the world. One does not have to engage in religious rituals, belong to a church or even believe in God to be spiritual . . . Identifying proxies for spirituality is more difficult because of its highly individual and personal nature. Such proxies include the extent of prayer or meditation, importance individuals attach to their spiritual life and personal statements linked to purpose in life and hope for the future.

People can be declared Atheists, yet if they have a positive outlook on life, *i.e.* have decided their life has meaning and purpose, and they hope to make the world a better place, this survey would count them as "religious or spiritual."

By creating such a positive and all-inclusive definition of what constitutes "religious or spiritual," the group that remains, the vehemently "non-religious," becomes an extremely depressed and negative sub-group of the population. In almost every case, this study compares this small, negativistic subgroup to those who attend church weekly or more often, and to whom religious belief is very important. I would submit that few Americans fall into either of these groups.

The ARIS survey tells us that 14% of the adult population is non-religious and at least another 40% don't attend services. You would expect the CASA "non-religious" group to reflect these percentages. However, when the CASA survey compares alcohol use among those who think religion is very important *versus* those who strongly disagree that religion is important, the CASA survey admits that this "non-religious" comparison group represents only 3% of the population. The data are further skewed because the respondents are not asked if they feel religion in general is important or not, but are asked whether they feel their religious views are important. Even totally secular Atheists would be likely to answer that they felt their religious views are important; so, once again, the remaining group who feel strongly that their own religious views are unimportant is a very negativistic subgroup, and are expressing views consistent with the low self-esteem and negative self-image that often accompanies substance abuse. By crafting this subgroup for its comparisons, the CASA survey guarantees that the more positive and inclusive "religious" group will have lower rates of substance abuse.

Distorting Use and Abuse

The third clue that this report is distorting its findings is found in how they defined the problem. The report is full of statements that seem to reflect serious health problems. For example: "Adults who never attend religious services are almost twice as likely to drink as those who attend religious services weekly or more often," and "91% of women over age 59 who do not identify themselves as religious consume alcohol." Yes, both sentences are about alcohol use, and contain fancy scientific and statistical jargon, but what are they really talking about here? *The definition of alcohol abuse in this case is having had one drink in the past month.* Even your humble author can admit to having had a glass of wine with dinner at least once in the past month. I don't feel this represents a national health crisis worthy of statistical analysis.

A more disturbing statistic is CASA's claim that 24% of those who never attend religious services reported having five or more drinks on one occasion in the past month.

However, in a footnote, the researchers note that many of these problem drinkers could be college students, especially those in fraternities. They also admit that while those who have little or no interest in religion drink alcohol and party more frequently than their religious peers, *the rates of alcoholism do not differ between the groups.*

A final fatal flaw in this report is the fact that no multivariate analysis was done. When assessing the relationship between any two variables, say alcohol consumption and religious belief, you must ascertain if you are actually measuring something other than the target variable. For example, if you are looking at the relationship between church attendance and alcohol consumption, you might find that those who attend church drink less than those who do not. If your goal was to belittle those who are non-believers, you would probably stop right there and publish your report. But if you are interested in a deeper understanding of the issue, you would subject your data to multivariate analysis—and what you might find is that it is not that people who attend church drink less, it is people who are married drink less. The fact that married people tend to be churchgoers is interesting, but it is unrelated to the original research question.

According to the ARIS survey, non-believers have a high rate of being single or unmarried. Analysis might have shown that the seemingly high rate of substance abuse in the CASA non-believer category was actually related to the group's marital status, rather than having anything to do with their lack of religious belief. A similar confounding variable is age. The ARIS survey notes that over one-third of the non-religious are between 18 and 29 years of age. Experimentation with drugs and alcohol tends to occur at this age. Sometimes discovering how much alcohol is the right amount entails repeated episodes of finding out how much is too much. Multivariate analysis might have shown that it was the relative youth of the non-believer group that was the critical variable, not their religious beliefs. But the CASA researchers did no such analysis.

Like every Templeton-funded research project before it, this latest report suffers from researcher bias. From the title "So Help Me God," to the fact that "God" as an actual entity is consistently cited as important to addicts' treatment (rather than a "belief in God") this report exhibits a religious, rather than scientific, slant on the research. It used inflated figures for religious belief, arbitrarily created misleading categories to skew the results, and in many cases exaggerated the severity of the issues being studied. Its conclusions are misleading and biased toward faith-based solutions.

Do some people benefit from religiously based substance abuse programs such as AA [Alcoholic Anonymous] and NA [Narcotics Anonymous]? Of course. They are helpful to many, and should be continued. Should priests, pastors and rabbis learn more about substance abuse and its treatment? Yes. Educating all community leaders on substance abuse issues and treatment is a good idea.

But it is a significant violation of the public trust when a University research center compromises its research in order to appease a funding organization, especially when subsequent public policy decisions could affect peoples' lives. Where the CASA report specifically fails the public is in not demanding more non-religious interventions for drug and alcohol abuse. It is difficult to find rational, non-religious alternatives to AA and NA Rescue Missions are often sponsored by religious organizations. And while I disagree with the CASA report on the extent to which this problem affects the non-believer population, substance abuse is a problem in our society, and with the number of non-religious adults increasing dramatically (more than doubling in the past ten years), it is imperative to find ways to reach this group with education and treatment options which they can accept. The vast majority of adults in this country are not going to be reached by having sermons on substance abuse preached from the pulpit since they are not going to be in church in the first place. In Oregon, Washington, Idaho and Wyoming the non-religious are now the largest denomination in the state. We need to spend more of our resources on secular alternatives to religiously based support and treatment options—not only for addiction, but also for the homeless, the hungry, pregnant teens, and at-risk youth. No one should be forced to pray or profess a belief in a higher power, in order to receive a meal, obtain medical treatment, or join a support group to maintain sobriety. It is simply un-American.

"A National Institutes of Health (NIH) consensus development panel concluded that methadone maintenance is the most effective treatment for opioid addiction."

Methadone Maintenance Is an Effective Treatment for Heroin Addiction

Sharon Stancliff

Because heroin addiction is a physiological condition that alters the brain's chemistry, simply abstaining is difficult for heroin addicts, claims Sharon Stancliff in the following viewpoint. An effective alternative to abstinence, she argues, is long-term methadone maintenance. According to the author, methadone, an opiate drug administered to addicts in order to eliminate their craving for heroin, has no significant adverse side effects and can reduce the risk addicts will become infected with the human immunodeficiency virus (HIV) from unclean needles. Stancliff is the medical director of the Harlem East Life Plan Methadone Maintenance Treatment Program in New York City.

As you read, consider the following questions:
1. According to Stancliff, what changes have scientists observed in the brain chemistry of heroin addicts?
2. In the author's view, why do many patients have no access to methadone maintenance treatment?
3. Why do heroin addicts sometimes require a great deal of education about the benefits of methadone treatment, in the author's view?

Sharon Stancliff, "Methadone Maintenance," *American Family Physician*, vol. 63, June 15, 2001, p. 2,335. Copyright © 2001 by *American Family Physician*. Reproduced by permission.

The development of addiction remains poorly understood, but evidence now supports the proposition that opioid addiction has a physiologic basis influenced by both genetics and the environment. Much addiction research has focused on an apparent "reward pathway" of the mesolimbic system, where opioid-mediated dopamine pathways help to generate the positive-feedback system that supports species-sustaining activities such as eating and procreation. The central role of endogenous opioids to this system suggests the mechanism by which the drive to administer exogenous opioids can become as intense as the drives for food and sex.

Changes that have been observed in association with chronic administration of opioids include physical atrophy of dopamine-producing neurons in the ventral tegmental area.[1] Such changes may account for some of the aversive symptoms of opioid withdrawal. It is theorized that neuroadaptations to chronic drug exposure may also lead to the long-term anhedonia[2] that many opioid users experience and may explain why sustained abstinence is so difficult for many users.

An Effective Treatment

In 1997, a National Institutes of Health (NIH) consensus development panel concluded that methadone maintenance is the most effective treatment for opioid addiction. Methadone is initiated at 20 to 40 mg and gradually increased until the patient reports clinical comfort and urine screens are free of other opioids. Most studies suggest that patients generally require a methadone dosage of 60 to 120 mg per day to stop using and craving heroin, although some patients respond to lower dosages and others require much higher dosages.

Methadone maintenance is a long-term therapy. The majority of patients who discontinue methadone relapse to heroin use, and no factors reliably predict which opioid-dependent patients may do well without pharmacotherapy. Long-term methadone treatment has no major adverse effects. Constipation and increased sweating are the most common side effects, and they tend to diminish over time. Be-

1. part of the midbrain that releases dopamine, a chemical that stimulates the positive reinforcement or reward center   2. the absence of pleasure or the ability to experience it

cause methadone can be used safely during pregnancy, it is the treatment of choice in opioid-dependent pregnant women. Physicians need to be aware of methadone's interactions with other drugs and should be alert for information about possible interactions as new medications are introduced.

An Effective Treatment for Heroin Addiction

Methadone is to heroin users what nicotine skin patches are to tobacco smokers. Both deliver "addictive" drugs—albeit drugs that pose virtually no health risks—in a form designed to reduce associated harms to consumers and others. Both have proven effective in reducing more dangerous forms of drug consumption. Both are readily integrated with most living styles. Consumed orally or transdermally, neither provides addicts with much of the effect on mood or cognition that is experienced with injected heroin or smoked cigarettes. But both are potentially available in other forms—injections, nasal sprays, and inhalers—that may be more effective for some users.

Ethan Nadelmann and Jennifer McNeely, *Public Interest*, Spring 1996.

Studies have found that persons on methadone maintenance are three to six times less likely to become infected with the human immunodeficiency virus (HIV), even if they continue to use drugs. One study compared heroin addicts who were receiving methadone maintenance treatment with heroin addicts who were not receiving this treatment. Follow-up of HIV-negative patients over 18 months showed seroconversion rates of 3.5 percent among those who remained on methadone versus 22 percent among those who were not treated with methadone. Heroin addicts who are already infected with HIV also benefit from methadone treatment. One study found that HIV-positive patients with a history of heroin addiction who were receiving methadone maintenance were less likely to be hospitalized than their counterparts who were not taking methadone.

Regulations require frequent attendance at methadone programs, and the number of methadone maintenance spots is highly restricted. Many patients are required to attend six to seven days per week, and only after three years can patients who are considered to be socially rehabilitated decrease their attendance to weekly. Thus, many patients have no access to treatment, and others are deterred by the strict regulations. The NIH Consensus Report stated, "The unnecessary regulations of methadone maintenance therapy and other long-acting opiate agonist[3] treatment programs should be reduced, and coverage for these programs should be a required benefit in public and private insurance programs." In March 2001, the federal regulations were modified, allowing more liberal take-home privileges. Each state has the option of adopting these regulations.

As [L.L.] Krambeer [W. von McKnelly Jr., W.F. Gabrielli, Jr., and E.C. Penick] note in their article on methadone therapy, which appears in [the June 15, 2001], issue of *American Family Physician*, there is a move toward a greater role for office-based prescribing, also termed "office-based opioid therapy." In New York City, a highly successful pilot project has been operating for more than 15 years. A federal waiver allows stable patients to participate in "medical maintenance" through monthly visits to a primary care physician, from whom they receive methadone in addition to regular medical care.

Until office-based prescribing becomes common, primary care physicians can play a supportive role in methadone therapy. Because methadone use is highly stigmatized, opioid addicts may require a great deal of education about the benefits of this treatment. Because misconceptions about methadone are widespread, it may be helpful to include family members in educational efforts. Krambeer and associates suggest that patients become involved in Narcotics Anonymous (NA); however, NA and other similar programs often consider methadone maintenance to be contrary to recovery. In becoming knowledgeable about methadone as a treatment for opioid dependence, the primary care physician can play an important role in bringing this highly effective modality to its full potential.

3. a chemical that combined with a cell receptor can reproduce a physiological reaction typical of a naturally occurring substance

"Methadone is not the answer."

Methadone Maintenance Programs Are Abused by Heroin Addicts

I.E. Hawksworth

In the following viewpoint, originally published as a letter addressed to the editor of the *Abbotsford Times*, I.E. Hawksworth, a former addict who works with heroin addicts in prison, argues that methadone is not the answer to the problem of heroin addiction. Many on the methadone program, which administers methadone to addicts in order to eliminate their craving for heroin, continue to use heroin, he claims. He also contends that many addicts abuse the methadone program by doing whatever it takes, including submitting other people's urine for testing, to get enough methadone to induce a high. Rather than support a system that promotes addiction, Hawksworth maintains, money should be spent on programs that build an addict's self-worth.

As you read, consider the following questions:
1. According to Hawksworth, why would addicts only use half the dose of methadone they were given at a clinic?
2. In the author's view, what policies contradict the belief that methadone stops criminals from doing crime?
3. What other program, in addition to methadone, encourages abuse by the addicts who use it, in Hawksworth's opinion?

I.E. Hawksworth, "Former Addict Says Methadone Not the Answer," *Abbotsford Times*, vol. 283, February 22, 2003. Copyright © 2003 by *Abbotsford Times*. Reproduced by permission.

I used heroin for many years of my life, as well as many other drugs. I knew many people on the methadone program. Whenever I was sick and could not find heroin, I would go down to the methadone clinic and wait until someone came out with a "carry" [take-home supply of methadone] and buy their methadone at $1 per milligram, 50 milligrams for $50.

A Long List of Abuses

Some friends would get on the program, get their doses raised every week until they were on the maximum dose. Depending on what doctor they were seeing, that maximum could be anywhere from 120 mg to 250 mg.

Once they were at the maximum they would then bring themselves down without letting their doctors know. They would only be using half of what they were given and sell the rest.

When they had to drink the full dose in front of the pharmacist, they would leave the drug store, stick their fingers down their throat and purge so they would not overdose on the high dose.

Most of the people I knew also continued using while on the methadone program, and in order to beat the urine analysis they would have someone urinate in a cup, hand that in, and the test result would be clean. They would actually buy someone else's urine. People in this community are led to believe that methadone stops criminals from doing crime. If that is true, why is it that they have the policy in place, that when someone on the methadone program ends up with such serious charges that they are sentenced to do jail time, they are automatically given their methadone in jail?

From the other side the frustration I felt was working with people in prison applying for parole. A lot of the prisoners were told that they would not receive parole unless they went on the methadone program, even after being drug free. Methadone is the worst drug to detox from. It is so severe that even the licensed detox centres will not even attempt the process without the individual being down to a minimum of 30 mg per day, which is a very low dose. When looking into the institutions that give methadone out to the prisoners, I know people that actually vomit methadone up after drinking it and then someone actually drinking that to reach the high.

The Madness of Methadone

Addicts like Scott P. contend that what clinics say they do and what is actually carried out by clinic administrators are two different things. "Methadone is probably the worst thing that can be given to somebody because you're saying it's okay to get high."

He claims that during his two years on a methadone program he never stopped using heroin, which was repeatedly revealed in urine test. . . . Most clients, he maintains, abuse the system. "I think the people like me were in the majority. I know people who were on three clinics at once."

Scott P. was eventually detoxed (he claims in four days), went through the prolonged painful withdrawal from methadone—consisting of convulsions, constant vomiting and bone aches—and went back to full-time heroin addiction to a much greater extent. He lived like this until he entered Springfield's Marathon House [in Massachusetts] two years ago, where he completed their one-year program and remains active in a 12-step program.

Keith Sikes, *Valley Advocate*, January 5, 1995.

In my opinion methadone is not the answer. Spend the money on opening a detox facility, . . . as well as more treatment facilities, recovery homes and safe homes for follow-up recovery.

When the needle exchange opened in Vancouver [Canada], I used to go around to the back alleys and pick up the old used needles and bring them in to exchange. After hours I could sell them for $2 a piece and use the money to get another fix. Fifty needles was $100.

When I had drugs and the needle exchange was not open, I used whatever needle was available. It didn't matter to me who used it before me. If I had bleach, I would rinse it; if not, I just cleaned it with water.

When I was looking to score drugs, I knew that a dealer would be not too far away from the exchange. When I was selling drugs, I knew that I could sell near the exchange. It didn't matter to me at the time that the police station was right across the street.

When you are wired out on drugs, your self-esteem is so low that you don't care if you live or die. Let's work on building the self-worth and start saving lives. Treatment works. Let's stick with what works. Drug addicts do recover, when led in the right direction.

*"Some problem drinkers can be trained to
control their intake."*

Some Problem Drinkers Can Drink in Moderation

Sally L. Satel

Some problem drinkers are not alcoholics and can learn to
control their intake of alcohol, claims Sally L. Satel in the
following viewpoint. Proponents of abstinence-only programs refuse to admit that there is a distinction between alcoholics and problem drinkers, and they erroneously claim
that all problem drinkers who reject abstinence are simply in
denial about their alcoholism; however, research shows that
some problem drinkers can in fact drink in moderation,
maintains Satel. To force problem drinkers to choose abstinence, she argues, denies many people the treatment they
need. Dr. Satel, a psychiatrist who works in a Washington
methadone clinic, is author of *PC, M.D.: How Political Cor-
rectness Is Corrupting Medicine.*

As you read, consider the following questions:
1. In Satel's view, what two events rekindled the
   controversy about treatment approaches that allow for
   some controlled drinking?
2. According to the U.S. government's National Household
   Survey, what is the working definition of the heavy
   drinker?
3. In the author's opinion, what are the warning signs that
   a problem drinker has crossed the line into alcoholism?

Sally L. Satel, "Learning to Say 'I've Had Enough,'" *New York Times*, July 14,
2000. Copyright © 2000 by The New York Times Company. Reproduced by
permission.

Can people who drink too much be taught to control their alcohol consumption? Unthinkable, say mainstream treatment organizations like the Betty Ford Center and Hazelden, which have long insisted on total abstinence.

Now controversy about a treatment approach that allows for some controlled drinking has flared again. [Early in July 2000], in Washington State, . . . a leading proponent of this option, Audrey Kishline, pleaded guilty to killing two people while driving drunk. She is the founder of Moderation Management, set up in 1993 as an alternative to the abstinence-only Alcoholics Anonymous. Then Alex DeLuca, the director of the respected Smithers Addiction Treatment and Research Center in New York City, resigned after failing to persuade his clinic to offer some alternative to total abstinence.

The case of Ms. Kishline may argue strongly against the idea, but some problem drinkers can be trained to control their intake. The difficulty is in figuring out which ones.

The working definition of the heavy drinker, according to the government's National Household Survey, is the consumption of five or more drinks on a single occasion, five or more times within a month. This kind of use, excessive as it is, doesn't make someone an alcoholic. A heavy drinker could be a college student who drinks to the point of getting sick on Saturday nights but keeps up his grades and football practice. Or an employee who drinks a bottle of wine alone at night but never misses a deadline.

Call these people "problem drinkers"—but not alcoholics. It is possible, but far from guaranteed, that they will become full-blown alcoholics, drinking compulsively despite serious consequences like deteriorating job performance and withdrawal symptoms.

The distinction between the problem drinker and the alcoholic, while not razor sharp, exists—but hard-core opponents of the drinking-in-moderation policy don't want to acknowledge it. To them, you are either an alcoholic or not. Virtually no treatment program will accept a patient who rejects abstinence as a goal. And counselors tend to engage in double-think: if the patient says he's an alcoholic, he is; if he refuses to admit he has a problem, he's an alcoholic "in denial" and headed toward the gutter.

But there are data that contradict this view. The "Handbook of Alcoholism Treatment Approaches," a textbook for clinicians, provides evidence that some problem drinkers can successfully control their consumption. Admittedly, this approach only works when the risks are relatively low. If an individual has crossed the line, admittedly fuzzy, into alcoholism, then the risks of allowing someone to have an occasional drink or two become too high.

The Advantages of Moderation Programs

By the time people reach serious stages of alcohol dependency, changing drinking becomes more difficult, and treatment is usually costly. MM [Moderation Management] believes that this situation needs to be remedied in the interest of public health and human kindness with early intervention and harm reduction programs. Moderation programs are less costly, shorter in duration, less intensive, and have higher success rates than traditional abstinence-only approaches.

Moderation Management, 2001.

The warning signs that the line has been crossed are a history of domestic violence, suicide attempts, missed work, neglected children—an "unmanageable" life in the words of Alcoholics Anonymous. Ms. Kishline must have known that the risks for her were too high because she had quit Moderation Management and joined Alcoholics Anonymous . . . several months before the fatal accident.

Advocates of total abstinence are afraid that some people will use the Moderation Management option as an excuse to drink. But the majority of problem drinkers, let alone alcoholics, have already rejected abstinence, Surveys from Alcoholics Anonymous indicate that its annual dropout rates average around 75 percent.

True, some doctors worry that sober recovering alcoholics will start to think that moderate drinking is O.K. and try it. The task for the therapist is to have the patient think hard about why he wants to sabotage so much. Some drinkers will never lose hope that they can one day enjoy alcohol minus the devastation, but the chances for relapse are reduced if we are adamant that controlled drinking is not an option for everybody.

At the same time, intolerance of moderate drinking also has a price.

"If some problem drinkers are told by treatment professionals that their choice is abstinence or no treatment, they will take nothing, and the opportunity to help is lost," says Jon Morgenstern, director of alcohol treatment research at the Mount Sinai School of Medicine in New York City.

So, the choice is rather stark. Admit that some problem drinkers aren't alcoholics, and help them learn how to drink moderately. Or insist on abstinence for those with even mild drinking problems—and drive millions of people away who need help.

> "*Moderation management is nothing but alcoholics covering up their problem.*"

Problem Drinkers Cannot Drink in Moderation

Mike Harden

In the following viewpoint Mike Harden maintains that problem drinkers cannot drink in moderation. The author cites, for example, the case of Audrey Kishline, who pled guilty to vehicular homicide in the drunk-driving deaths of a father and daughter. According to the author, Kishline was the leading proponent of Moderation Management, a program developed to help problem drinkers learn to drink in moderation. Kishline herself concluded that the program was simply a way for alcoholics to hide their problem, the author claims. Harden is a *Columbus Dispatch* columnist.

As you read, consider the following questions:
1. What analogy does Tom Pepper use to explain why controlled drinking is impossible for those with alcoholic drinking patterns?
2. According to Harden, what motivated Kishline to seek a less rigid way to address drinking issues?
3. For whom is Kishline's Moderation Management program intended, in Harden's view?

Mike Harden, "Author Now Knows Moderate Drinking Method Doesn't Work," *Columbus Dispatch*, July 3, 2000. Copyright © 2000 by *Columbus Dispatch*. Reproduced by permission.

S ix years ago, the mere mention of author Audrey Kish-line's book *Moderate Drinking* was enough to set the alcohol-treatment community on edge all the way from Manhattan to Maui.

"I met the lady and debated her on television before," said Dr. Tom Pepper, medical director of Talbot Hall, Ohio State University's alcohol and chemical dependency treatment center.

Kishline was a proponent of the notion that problem drinkers could teach themselves to drink socially once again by following her "nine steps toward moderation and balance."

A Controversial Plan

Her book, subtitled *The Moderation Management Guide for People Who Want to Reduce Their Drinking*, made her a much-sought-after subject for talk shows. *Psychology Today* show-cased her controversial plan in a cover article that appeared after publication of *Moderate Drinking*. Kishline argued that self-imposed behavior modification techniques are sufficient to corral unmanaged drinking patterns. She said such tech-niques spare individuals the ordeal of treatment and lifelong consignment to an abstinence-based recovery program.

"I don't know of any credible organization or publication that recommends controlled drinking for people with alco-holic drinking patterns," Pepper said. "You can make a pickle out of a cucumber, but you can't make a cucumber out of a pickle. Controlled drinking is that attempt to unpickle the cucumber."

Kishline believed otherwise. She suggested that her per-sonal experiences with the 12-step program of Alcoholics Anonymous had left her wanting for a less rigid way to address drinking issues. Promotional copy heralding publication of her book noted, "Based on her own unsatisfactory experience with abstinence-based programs, Kishline offers inspiration and a step-by-step program to help individuals avoid the kind of drinking that detrimentally affects their lives."

Her Web site for Moderation Management explained, "MM is intended for problem drinkers who have experi-enced mild-to-moderate levels of alcohol-related problems."

Jill Reese, a Talbot Hall staff member, has observed attempts to make social drinkers of people with significant alcohol-related problems. "I've worked in this field for 20 years, and I've never met anybody who could pull it off."

No Way Back for Alcoholics

John Schwarzlose, president, Betty Ford Center: The reason we have movements like Moderation Management is because of the confusion that is overwhelming about alcohol and alcoholism in our society. In reality, there is well-defined criteria that distinguishes between the abuse of alcohol and alcoholism.

Once someone is addicted to alcohol, is an alcoholic, there is a change, an alteration, of the neurochemistry of the brain. And you cannot go back once you've become addicted to that drug.

John Schwarzlose, CNN.com, July 10, 2000.

After basking in the talk-show limelight, Kishline faded from public controversy and—so it seemed—became less a thorn in the side of alcohol-treatment experts.

A Tragic Awakening

Not many days ago [on June 20, 2000], however, she was the subject of a news release prepared by the National Council on Alcoholism and Drug Dependence. The release was issued on the day Kishline, 43, was scheduled to go to trial on two counts of vehicular manslaughter in Washington state.

According to police reports and news accounts, Kishline on March 25 [2000] was driving her pickup truck in the wrong direction on Washington's I-90. She struck a vehicle driven by Richard Davis of Yakima County.

Davis was killed instantly. His 12-year-old daughter, LaSchell, died before reaching the hospital.

Kishline's blood-alcohol level was measured at 0.26 following the crash, a reading which—in Washington—is more than three times the legal limit. She was hospitalized briefly for chest and facial injuries.

Two months before the fatal crash, Kishline apparently had experienced second thoughts about her personal issues with alcohol. She announced on her Web site that she was stepping down as Moderation Management's spokeswoman and giving up moderation drinking for abstinence.

Kishline wept as she pleaded guilty on Thursday [June 29, 2000] to two counts of vehicular homicide in the deaths of Davis and his daughter. Kishline's lawyer told a Seattle journalist that his client is "extremely remorseful" and that she had carried photographs of the two crash victims with her at an alcohol treatment center.

Sources said Kishline conceded that "moderation management is nothing but alcoholics covering up their problem."

That admission doesn't come as news to Tom Pepper or Jill Reese any more than it does to the National Council on Alcoholism and Drug Dependence.

Would that the price of Kishline's awakening were consequences that only she had to deal with.

Periodical Bibliography

The following articles have been selected to supplement the diverse views presented in this chapter.

David Farabee	"Addicted to Treatment," *Forbes*, December 23, 2002.
Steve Friedman	"One More Round: Can an Alcoholic Who's Been Sober for 17 Years Leap Off the Wagon into the Risky Realm of Moderation?" *Men's Health*, May 2003.
Keith Humphreys	"Can Addiction-Related Self-Help/Mutual-Aid Groups Lower Demand for Professional Substance Abuse Treatment?" *Social Policy*, Winter 1998.
Linda Davis Kyle	"Alternative Treatments for Addictions: Promises and Perils," *Counselor*, August 1999.
David Lewis	"Drug-Assisted Addiction Treatment: Stop the Discrimination," *Brown University Digest of Addiction Theory and Application*, December 2000.
Charles Marwick	"Treatment Works for Substance Abusers," *JAMA*, October 7, 1998.
Sharon O'Hara	"Injecting Hope," *Community Care*, May 2, 2002.
Tara Parker-Pope	"Kicking the Habit (Sort of): New Theory Lets Smokers Smoke, Alcoholics Drink," *Wall Street Journal*, July 2, 2002.
Stanton Peele	"Drunk with Power: The Case Against Court-Imposed 12-Step Treatments," *Reason*, May 2001.
Stanton Peele	"Everything in Moderation: The Debate over Alcohol: Is One Too Many?" *Star Ledger*, August 13, 2000.
Richard Sadovsky	"Public Health Issue: Methadone Maintenance Therapy," *American Family Physician*, July 15, 2000.
Gerald D. Shulman	"Addiction Treatment 'Success' Is Killing Us," *Behavioral Health Management*, September/October 2002.
Harold Sloves	"Drug Treatment for Drug Addiction: Surmounting the Barriers," *Behavioral Health Management*, July 2000.

Abraham J. Twerski   "Comic Relief: Cartoons Can Often Succeed
                      Where Therapists Fail," *Professional Counselor*,
                      April 1998.

Lawrence Matthew   "Faith Communities Have Powerful Influence
Ventline   in Confronting Addictions," *Counselor*, October
                      2002.

Clare Wilson   "Fixed Up: When Nothing Else Works,
                      Heroin Addicts Should Be Prescribed the Drug
                      They Crave," *New Scientist*, March 30, 2002.

CHAPTER 4

How Should the Government Deal with Addiction?

Chapter Preface

State-sponsored lotteries and the controversy over their impact are nothing new in the United States. In fact, an English lottery supported the first American settlement in Jamestown, Virginia, in 1612. Despite opposition by those colonists who saw gambling as a dangerous activity that encouraged immoral behavior, all thirteen original colonies held lotteries to raise revenue. By 1894, however, gambling was considered a corrupting influence and was banned in most states. The tide turned once again in 1964 when the citizens of New Hampshire, who paid no sales or income tax, approved a state-sponsored lottery to raise funds needed for education. The idea of using lotteries to raise state revenues slowly spread among the states, and by December 2002, thirty-nine states had sponsored lotteries. One of several arguments against these lotteries is that they promote addictive gambling. Those who subscribe to this view argue that all people are vulnerable to compulsive gambling; thus the promotion of state-sponsored lotteries should be regulated. Others believe that the benefits derived from state lotteries outweigh the harm to a minority of gamblers who do so compulsively.

Those who support state-sponsored lotteries argue that compulsive gamblers constitute a minority of those who choose to gamble. A Harvard Medical School study found that only 1.6 percent of gamblers were considered "clinically disordered," which supports this assumption. Moreover, supporters claim, lotteries generate substantial income for the states that sponsor them. In 1999 total U.S. lottery sales totaled $3.7 billion. States use this lottery revenue to benefit their citizens in a variety of ways. In California, lottery funds support education and in Colorado, funds are used to preserve wildlife and open space. Lottery advocates conclude that the benefits to the people of states that vote to accept lotteries outweigh the risk to the few.

Opponents contend that compulsive gambling is a vulnerability common to everyone, and state-sponsored lotteries take advantage of these natural weaknesses. Valerie C. Lorenz, an expert on pathological gambling, believes that the reintroduction of the lottery has made Americans more accepting of gambling, thus facilitating the legalization of other gambling activities and encouraging a supply of future gamblers. The outcomes for compulsive gamblers and their families can be devastating. "They become so out of control," Lorenz maintains. "When someone drinks too much, at some point they pass out. If someone gambles to the point of being out of control, they will try to win it back. They chase their losses, and in a 48-hour period the losses can become huge."

Those hoping to protect these vulnerable citizens argue that state governments must discontinue their predatory advertising practices. According to the authors of *National Issues Forums*, states spend $370 million a year on advertising campaigns to coax the most vulnerable people into buying lottery tickets. In Washington State, the authors reveal for example, lottery ads coincide with the delivery of Social Security and welfare checks. In one poverty-stricken Chicago neighborhood, the authors write, a billboard reads, "This Could Be Your Ticket Out." According to business professor Julian Simon, this behavior is not only reprehensible, but hypocritical:

> Government nowadays is not only willing to profit from people's betting, but also to promote it. This is extraordinarily sinful, in my view. What the government formerly hunted down with the police and courts when done privately, it now not only tolerates but actively engenders—simply because government and officials benefit. Even worse are the diabolical devices appealing to the fantasies of have-nots with the hope of huge hits. If there ever was a get-rich-quick scam, this is it—perpetrated by government. All in the "public interest," of course.

Whether or not state lotteries and the advertising used to promote them encourage addictive gambling is controversial. The authors of the viewpoints in the following chapter examine whether or not the government should intervene to reduce the problem of addiction.

"Congress must act now to clearly and unequivocally ban Internet gambling."

Internet Gambling Should Be Banned

Richard Blumenthal

In the following viewpoint Connecticut's attorney general, Richard Blumenthal, claims that Internet gambling interests take advantage of gambling addicts, who find it easier to hide their addiction by using the Internet as opposed to more traditional gambling methods, such as buying lottery tickets. Blumenthal argues that Congress should prohibit all Internet gambling and the use of financial instruments—such as credit and debit cards—when used to finance online gambling. By granting law enforcement broad powers to prosecute those who violate these laws, Blumenthal contends, the government can send a clear message that the United States will not tolerate Internet gambling.

As you read, consider the following questions:
1. In addition to taking advantage of gambling addicts, what are some of the other problems associated with Internet gambling, in Blumenthal's view?
2. In the author's opinion, what would prohibiting the use of financial instruments such as credit and debit cards prevent online gambling businesses from seeking?
3. What legislative proposals does Blumenthal include when he says Internet bans must admit no exceptions?

Richard Blumenthal, testimony before the Senate Committee on Banking, Housing and Urban Affairs, Washington, DC, March 18, 2003.

Use of the Web to place bets on the starting date of a war with Iraq speaks volumes about the sordid, despicable nature of an unregulated, faceless, nameless Internet gambling industry. Internet gambling is growing. Beginning with the first internet gambling website in 1995, the industry has exploded—Bear, Stearns estimates—to more than $8 billion in revenues in 2002.

Now, without delay, clear and specific federal measures are vital to add deterrent strength to current general prohibitions. State and federal law enforcement authorities have the historic opportunity and obligation to work together and halt the ongoing abuse.

The Threat of Internet Gambling

Internet gambling threatens the integrity of our athletic and sports institutions—from college basketball to professional football. It turns homes into betting parlors and lures bettors with pop-up advertising. If bettors finally stop playing—typically after losing thousands of dollars or maybe even after seeking counseling for gambling addiction—the industry barrages them with personal emails.

A 2002 study by the University of Connecticut found that Internet gamblers are most likely to develop signs of problem gambling. The anonymity of Internet gambling makes it easier for problem gamblers to conceal their activity. These addicted gamblers do not have to explain the hours spent at a casino or OTB [Off Track Betting] parlor or face a store owner every day while purchasing hundreds of dollars in instant lottery tickets.

A Need for Federal Laws

Congress must act now to clearly and unequivocally ban Internet gambling. There are a number of federal laws—including the Federal Wire Act, 18 USC 1084,—that provide a legal basis for prosecuting Internet gambling web sites located within the United States. In fact, several years ago, a successful prosecution was upheld involving the use of the Internet for sports betting: *U.S. v. Cohen*, 260 F.3d 68 (2nd Cir. 1999). The presence of these laws has been enough to prevent any organization from establishing a gambling web site based in our country. There is still a need for Congress to make the prohibition clear and unassailable.

Congress should enact provisions prohibiting the use of credit cards, debit cards, checks and other financial instruments for the purposes of Internet gambling. As in our battle against money laundering and terrorism, we must take steps to eradicate the financial infrastructure for this illegal activity. If federal law prohibits the use of credit cards and other financial instruments for Internet gambling, financial institutions are in a stronger position to reject any charge from such sources.

A Threat to the Nation

Problem gambling results in broken families, bankruptcy, crime and higher rates of suicide. Unlike "traditional" gambling, Internet gambling comes right into our homes, and thus carries an even greater ability to hurt a wider segment of the population. . . .

Illegal Internet gambling has reached epidemic proportions. Increasingly, it is putting our youth at greater risk, exacerbating pathological gambling, and opening the door for fraud and money laundering. It is a threat to our nation and must be stopped.

Spencer Bachus, "Don't Bet on It," http://bachus.house.gov, October 1, 2002.

In fact, Citibank, Discover, American Express, PayPal and others have already announced that they will not accept charges from online gambling facilities. A federal law would ensure full industry-wide compliance with this common sense policy. It would also prevent any on-line gambling business from seeking a court order for such payments. Without American dollars flowing through our credit card and debit card facilities, Internet gambling companies will be stunted if not stifled.

A Broad Application

Any new federal law must include federal and state enforcement provisions as well as criminal and civil sanctions. Because of the international and interstate nature of the Internet, federal criminal and civil enforcement is critical to the success of a law prohibiting Internet gaming and the use of credit and debit cards. States also must have enforcement authority. Many federal consumer protection laws include authorization for state attorneys general to bring civil actions against violators of federal law. This state enforcement role often meaningfully supplements federal enforcement efforts and leads to greater compliance with the law's provisions.

Finally, any ban on Internet gambling and the use of financial instruments in furtherance of such gambling must be clear and broad, admitting no exceptions. I oppose legislative proposals authorizing the use of the Internet for state sanctioned gambling. These exceptions would almost certainly encourage states to use the Internet for state lotteries, OTB and other gaming. These exceptions swallow the rule, leading to the use of credit card and debit cards to fund purchases of state lottery tickets and for other state gambling.

Currently, no state, except for California's Off Track Betting game, uses the Internet for state gaming. Few states allow use of credit and debit cards to pay for state lottery tickets and other games. An exception may create more problems by encouraging people to play on the Internet and use credit or debit cards to fund excessive gambling, creating crushing personal debt and tragedy.

Congress should take the simple, straightforward approach: prohibit all online gambling and prohibit the use of credit and debit cards and other financial instruments for Internet gambling.

*"A ban on Internet gambling violates our
natural and Constitutional rights."*

Internet Gambling Should Not Be Banned

Fred E. Foldvary

According to Fred E. Foldvary in the following viewpoint, individuals should be free to choose whether or not they want to gamble on the Internet without interference by the government. Claims that Internet gambling funds terrorism and threatens American consumers—used to garner support for a ban on Internet gambling—are exaggerated, he claims. Moreover, Foldvary argues, to ban Internet gambling would give the government the power to invade people's privacy and interfere with free enterprise. Fred E. Foldvary is senior editor of *Progress Report*, a libertarian publication.

As you read, consider the following questions:
1. In Foldvary's opinion, what would have been the effect of including an antigambling provision in an anti-terrorist bill?
2. What does the wide popularity of gambling indicate, in the author's view?
3. According to Foldvary, on what should an effective Internet gaming policy focus?

Fred E. Foldvary, "Keep Internet Gambling Legal," *Progress Report*, March 24, 2003. Copyright © 2003 by Fred E. Foldvary. Reproduced by permission.

The gambling industry, or "gaming" as they like to call it, has become a major player in the Internet. While real-estate–based casinos offer a lot of hardware such as slot machines, roulette wheels, and card tables, gambling is essentially a mental construct. The money that is exchanged is basically numbers, the vehicles such as cards and wheels are images that can be electronic, and the communication can now be digital. So gambling, like music and text, is well suited to doing business on the Internet.

Whereas many U.S. State governments ban gambling, other than their own lottery monopolies, the Internet has no real location, so online gambling slips by orthogonal to State and federal laws. Now some State legislators and Representatives in Congress are seeking to prohibit Internet gaming. Congressman James Leach of Iowa has been trying to enact his Unlawful Internet Gambling Funding Prohibition Act. The bill would make it illegal to send funds electronically for illegal online gambling.

Attempts to Ban Internet Gambling

The September 11 [2001], terrorist attacks have become for some an excuse to increase government power. Leach slipped his bill into an anti-terrorist bill. The excuse is that illegal Internet gambling web sites may have been used for money laundering by organized crime, and also, "Islamic" extremists have used money laundering in connection with their attacks. Leach combined these activities to allege that terrorists use Internet gambling to launder money.

But the FBI as well as the CIA have stated that there is no evidence that Islamic terrorists have had any connection with Internet gaming. The Senate voted for an anti-terrorist bill that did not include any prohibition of online gambling or its use of funds. The inclusion of the anti-gambling provisions would have complicated the bill unnecessarily at a time of crisis.

Representative Frank Wolf of Virginia has also called for bans on Internet gaming. According to I. Nelson Rose's article "Politics and the Law of Gambling" in the Spring 2002 *Gambling Times*, Wolf stated, "Gambling is beginning to destroy and fundamentally corrupt this country." Is he crying wolf?

At the State level, in California, Assemblyman Dario Frommer is pushing AB1229, a bill to ban Internet gambling in the State. If it becomes illegal for any resident in the State to gamble on the Internet, how is this supposed to be enforced? Is the State government to spy and monitor all Internet messages coming into and out of the State? The bill passed the State Assembly 61-2 but has so far not been passed by the California Senate. *Gambling Times* reports that their telephone calls to him have been ignored.

Spying on Private Computers

Assuming you were gambling on the Internet, how would the government ever know about it? For the government to know about such personal, consensual behavior requires spying. And that's what anti-gambling legislation would require. Banks and Internet Service Providers would be drafted into the role of snooper, sifting all financial transactions. The notion of government mandating surveillance of private computers is repugnant.

Clyde Wayne Crews, "Should Washington Ban Internet Gambling?" CNSNews.com, June 10, 2002.

One wonders what great problem these bills are trying to solve. Gambling does have its problems, including fraud and addiction, but the wide popularity of gambling indicates that most folks do not abhor it as some horrible sin or a great threat to national security.

The Dangers of Prohibition

A ban on Internet gambling violates our natural and Constitutional rights. If you are not allowed to indulge in gambling even inside your own home, then the government voids your property rights to your home as well as your right to spend your money as you wish. To enforce the law, the State would have to be given the power to intrude into your private conversations and financial dealings. Our rights have already been severely eroded as it is.

If there is a problem with fraud or other consumer protection, that can well be handled without a complete prohibition. And to the extent that online gambling takes away business from landed gaming places, the answer is that competition is not and should not be a tort or crime.

This is not to say that gambling is any wonderful thing. I personally think folks should have more productive and more wholesome ways of spending their time and money. But that's my personal taste. As a libertarian, I don't favor forcing anyone's personal preferences on others.

Life has enough risks and gambles without adding to them. But if folks like the thrill of taking chances with their money, to forcibly prevent them from doing so is an assault on their dignity as adult human beings with minds and values of their own. Whatever troubles exist with gaming, the best policy is to focus directly on the problem and not the medium or an activity that many indulge in without problems.

A ban on Internet gambling is not just a big-government nanny-state meddling with a recreational preference, but also a trade barrier, an intervention on enterprise, an assault on an industry. Shame on those legislatures who ignorantly wield their power against individual choice. They are the problem, not the gamblers.

> "Legalizers overstate the social costs of
> [illegal drug] prohibition, just as they
> understate the social costs of legalization."

Drug Laws Decrease Addiction

John P. Walters

In the following viewpoint John P. Walters argues that the prohibition of illegal drugs protects public health. Walters refutes the claim that prisons are flooded with innocent drug users, maintaining that most of those imprisoned are violent drug offenders. Walters also contests claims that legalization has worked in Europe, pointing out that Dutch decriminalization of marijuana has increased use by 300 percent. According to Walters, drugs, not drug laws, create problems for addicts and society. Walters is director of the National Office of Drug-Control Policy.

As you read, consider the following questions:

1. In Walters's opinion, what is the softest spot in the reasoning of legalizers?
2. In 1998 how much did American drug abuse cost, in the author's view?
3. According to Walters, what percentage of the child welfare caseload involves caregivers who abuse substances?

John P. Walters, "Don't Legalize Drugs," *Wall Street Journal*, July 19, 2002. Copyright © 2002 by Dow Jones & Company, Inc. All rights reserved. Reproduced by permission of the publisher and the author.

The charge that "nothing works" in the fight against illegal drugs has led some people to grasp at an apparent solution: legalize drugs. They will have taken false heart from news from Britain, . . . where the government acted to downgrade the possession of cannabis to the status of a non-arrestable offense.

According to the logic of the legalizers, it's laws against drug use, not the drugs themselves, that do the greatest harm. The real problem, according to them, is not that the young use drugs, but that drug laws distort supply and demand. Violent cartels arise, consumers overpay for a product of unknown quality, and society suffers when the law restrains those who "harm no one but themselves."

Better, the argument goes, for the government to control the trade in narcotics. That should drive down the prices (heroin would be "no more expensive than lettuce," argues one proponent), eliminate violence, provide tax revenue, reduce prison crowding, and foster supervised injection facilities.

Sounds good. But is it realistic? The softest spot in this line of reasoning is the analogy with alcohol abuse. The argument goes roughly like this: "Alcohol is legal. Alcohol can be abused. Therefore, cocaine should be legal." Their strongest argument, by contrast, is that prohibition produces more costs than benefits, while legalized drugs provide more benefits than costs.

The Social Costs

But legalizers overstate the social costs of prohibition, just as they understate the social costs of legalization. Take the statistic that more than 1.5 million Americans are arrested every year for drug crimes. Legalizers would have us believe that otherwise innocent people are being sent to prison (displacing "true" criminals) for merely toking up. But only a fraction of these arrestees are ever sentenced to prison. And there should be little question that most of those sentenced have earned their place behind bars.

Some 24% of state prison drug offenders are violent recidivists, while 83% have prior criminal histories. Only 17% are in prison for "first time offenses," while nominal "low-level" offenders are often criminals who plea-bargain to escape more serious charges. The reality is that a high percentage of all criminals, regardless of the offense, use drugs. In New York, 79% of those arrested for any crime tested positive for drugs.

Americans Spent $63 Billion on Illegal Drugs

Americans' overall spending on illegal drugs was an estimated $63.2 billion in 1999, a decline of $5.2 billion, or 7.6 percent, since 1997. Spending on cocaine dropped the most—by nearly $5 billion.

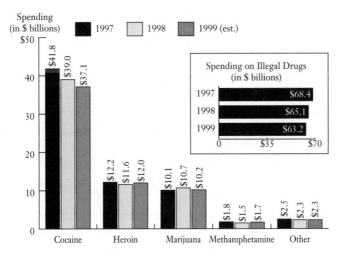

Office of National Drug Control Policy, 1999.

Drug abuse alone cost an estimated $55 billion in 1998 (excluding criminal justice costs), and deaths directly related to drug use have more than doubled since 1980. Would increasing this toll make for a healthier America? Legalization, by removing penalties and reducing price, would increase drug demand. Make something easier and cheaper to obtain, and you increase the number of people who will try it. Legalizers love to point out that the Dutch decriminalized marijuana in 1976, with little initial impact. But as drugs gained social acceptance, use increased consistently and sharply, with a 300% rise in use by 1996 among 18–20 year-olds.

Britain, too, provides an instructive example. When British

physicians were allowed to prescribe heroin to certain addicts, the number skyrocketed. From 68 British addicts in the program in 1960, the problem exploded to an estimated 20,000 heroin users in London alone by 1982.

Raising Questions

The idea that we can "solve" our complex drug problem by simply legalizing drugs raises more questions than it answers. For instance, what happens to the citizenship of those legally addicted? Will they have their full civil rights, such as voting? Can they be employed as school bus drivers? Nurses? What of a woman, legally addicted to cocaine, who becomes pregnant? Should she be constrained by the very government that provides for her habit?

Won't some addicts seek larger doses than those medically prescribed? Or seek to profit by selling their allotment to others, including minors? And what about those promised tax revenues—how do they materialize? As it is, European drug clinics aren't filled with productive citizens, but rather with demoralized zombies seeking a daily fix. Won't drugs become a disability entitlement?

Will legalization eliminate violence? The *New England Journal of Medicine* reported in 1999 on the risks for women injured in domestic violence. The most striking factor was a partner who used cocaine, which increased risk more than four times. That violence is associated not with drug laws, but with the drug. A 1999 report from the Department of Health and Human Services showed that two million children live with a parent who has a drug problem. Studies indicate that up to 80% of our child welfare caseload involves caregivers who abuse substances. Drug users do not harm only themselves.

Legalizers like to argue that government-supervised production and distribution of addictive drugs will eliminate the dangers attributed to drug prohibition. But when analyzing this "harm reduction" argument, consider the abuse of the opiate OxyContin, which has resulted in numerous deaths, physicians facing criminal charges, and addicts attacking pharmacies. OxyContin is a legally prescribed substance, with appropriate medical uses—that is, it satisfies those conditions legalizers envision for cocaine and heroin. The point is clear: The laws are not the problem.

Former Sen. Daniel Patrick Moynihan observed that drugs place us in a dilemma: "We are required to choose between a crime problem and a public health problem." Legalization is a dangerous mirage. To address a crime problem, we are asked to accept a public health crisis. Yet if we were to surrender, we would surely face both problems—intensified.

"Government regulation can result in harmful unintended consequences to the consumers of potentially addictive substances."

Drug Laws Increase Addiction

Adam Gifford

According to Adam Gifford in the following viewpoint, attempts to regulate addictive substances actually exacerbate problems associated with addiction. Gifford claims that regulation cannot alter the biological fact that when addicts are cut off from customary doses of an abused substance, their bodies will force them to find a substitute drug; thus when governments prohibit a drug, addicts find other, sometimes more harmful drugs of unknown quality and concentration. Gifford concludes that regulating addictive substances harms public health rather than improves it. Adam Gifford is a professor of economics at California State University at Northridge.

As you read, consider the following questions:
1. In Gifford's opinion, how is the activation of the reinforcement area of the brain by psychotropic substances different from activation by food?
2. How does the "set-point mechanism" operate in human smokers, in the author's view?
3. According to Gifford, what are some of the policy tools a state can use to regulate the consumption of a psychotropic substance?

Adam Gifford, "The Unintended Consequences of Regulating Addictive Substances," *Cato Journal*, vol. 18, Fall 1999, pp. 301–11. Copyright © 1999 by the Cato Institute. All rights reserved. Reproduced by permission.

Former Food and Drug Commissioner David Kessler, former Surgeon General C. Everett Koop, and a legion of others argue that significant government regulation is needed to protect consumers from nicotine, which has been shown to be addictive, and from smoking, which increases the risk of lung cancer, heart disease, and a host of other health problems. The biology and the economics of addiction, however, suggest that government regulation can result in harmful unintended consequences to the consumers of potentially addictive substances. . . .

The Motivation-Reinforcement System

Reinforcement of behavior depends on a goal-directed arousal system in the brain that is responsible for learning at a basic level, and this learning involves the creation of memories necessary for the survival of individuals and species. . . .

This motivational system allows creatures from bees to humans to take the measure of their environment in a very specific and sophisticated fashion. When an animal finds and consumes a good, a value—in economic terms, a marginal value—becomes attached to an internal representation of that good. This value is based on the ability of a good to enhance the fitness of an individual—that is, to increase the likelihood that an individual will survive and procreate. Furthermore, associations will be created between the good, its value, and characteristics such as location, complementary goods, and other environmental cues. In this example, the location where the good was found will be stored in memory, subject to recall when the animal seeks the good in the future. The associated goods and cues are used by the animal to predict when and where the primary reinforcing good can be found. Since the probability of finding a good in this same location in the future is uncertain, the motivational system enables the animal to form expectations about the probability of finding it there in the future. Expectations about associated or complementary cues and about the ability of a good to enhance fitness are formed and stored during a learning process, and the values attached to these expectations motivate behavior and generally allow the animal to organize that behavior in an efficient manner. The addictive properties of certain substances are a result of their effects on the motivation-reinforcement system.

Activating Reinforcement Systems

Addictive substances are defined as those that activate these reinforcing systems. However, the activation of the reinforcement area of the brain by psychotropic substances is generally different from its activation by ordinary reinforcing goods such as food. Food, for example, is only reinforcing when an animal is hungry—only a hungry animal will seek a location where, from past experience, it expects to find food. Addictive substances seem to be much more capable of reinforcement effects, independent of the animal's internal state. Also, the value assigned to an ordinary good reflects its expected ability to enhance the animal's fitness. The values assigned to potentially addictive goods may exceed the value that measures the ability of the good to satisfy these requirements.

The associated or complementary goods and cues by themselves will begin to activate the motivational area of the brain; they become conditioned reinforcers. These associations can be positive, as with the association of a good bottle of wine with a fine meal. The associations can also be adverse, such as when smoking and drinking alcohol become associated, making it difficult to quit one activity without quitting the other. Similarly, the sight of the needle used to inject heroin can become associated by reinforcement with the effects of the drug itself, so that simply seeing a needle can stimulate craving for the drug. And an associated location or social environment, for example, back alley needle sharing, can even become a sought-after aspect of the consumption of heroin.

The Set-Point Mechanism

In a recent set of experiments [S.H.] Ahmed and [G.F.] Koob (1998) found that rats allowed to self-administer cocaine "regulated their intoxication around some endogenous reference or 'hedonic set point.'" The initial consumption history, in part, determined the level of the set point. Animals given longer initial access periods to the drug escalated use over time and reached a higher set point then those with shorter access. For both low- and high-set-point animals "decreasing the [concentration of each] dose produced an increase in cocaine self-infusions," so that the rats could attain their set-point concentration levels in response to the diminished concentration of each dose. [According to M.L. Pianezza, E.M. Sellers, and R.F. Tyndale,] the same response has been seen in human smokers, where "dependent smokers adjust their smoking to maintain constant blood and brain nicotine concentrations."

Asay. © by *Colorado Springs Gazette Telegraph*. Reproduced by permission of Chuck Asay.

What the set-point response suggests for cigarette regulation is that if regulation mandated lower nicotine levels in cigarettes, individuals would simply adjust their smoking behavior to return their blood and brain nicotine concentrations to their set-point level by increasing the volume and depth of inhalations or the number of cigarettes smoked in a given period of time. The extent to which the smoker uses one or both of these methods to maintain nicotine concentration levels will depend on, among other factors, the economic costs of each method. Both methods will increase the harmful effects of smoking resulting from the absorption of nitrosamines, collectively referred to as tars, and from the absorption of carbon monoxide. Ironically, then, one of the results of reducing the nicotine levels in cigarettes is a potential increase in the injurious effects of smoking caused by tars and other harmful substances. It seems that this effect could, in part, be alleviated by reducing nitrosamine levels. However, it is primarily the tars that give cigarettes their taste and, in dependent smokers, that taste becomes associated with the pleasure of smoking by the reinforcing effects of nicotine. Like needle sharing, the associated taste becomes a feature of smoking sought after for its own sake. Consequently, reduced-tar cigarettes are not popular with smokers. In fact, it is possible that a set point for tar concentrations could result from the association effects of reinforcement. . . .

The Benefits of Addictive Substances

An often implicit assumption of those who argue in favor of the government regulation of addictive substances is that their consumption yields few or no benefits to the consumer. Though most economists reject this conclusion, I want to mention a few of the known biological benefits derived from consuming various psychotropic substances. One of the effects of many of these substances, including alcohol, barbiturates, heroin, tobacco, and marijuana, is that they reduce anxiety. Further, alcohol reduces inhibitions, and while this effect can sometimes result in trouble, by reducing social anxiety it probably increases the enjoyment of many individuals in certain social settings. Reduced cognitive activity is an effect related to the consumption of various psychotropic substances, and another suggested effect on individuals is short-term "myopia for the future."

All of these effects can be considered beneficial if not carried to the extreme, since they allow the individual a temporary respite from social anxieties and other cares, and they probably explain why most societies past and present have their equivalent of the six pack or glass of wine.

Interestingly, some substances can be said to increase cognitive ability by increasing alertness. Since some minimum level of alertness is necessary for rationality, substances like nicotine, caffeine, and even cocaine taken in small doses yield utility by increasing alertness and thus could be said actually to enhance rational thought. Of course, in larger doses cocaine can make users feel more rational and powerful than they actually are, and this can create problems. One of the interesting aspects of smoking is that there is evidence that it enhances memory formation and may be useful in enhancing the memories of Alzheimer's patients. Smoking may also result in a lower incidence of Parkinson's disease and can relieve some of its symptoms.

The Effects of Regulatory Policy

When the state makes the decision to regulate the consumption of a psychotropic substance, it has several policy tools it can use. It can use taxes, including taxes set so high that they drive legal provision to zero; it can use outright prohibition; and finally it can turn to a modern innovation—it can allow and encourage the use of the legal system to sue the legal producers of addictive substances out of the market. Increasing the "cost" of the legal consumption and production of potentially addictive substances by the various regulatory means will result in substitutions along several margins. . . .

A few examples will serve to illustrate the perverse effects of the state's attempt to regulate addictive substances. In 1644 the emperor of China banned the smoking of tobacco, which resulted in many Chinese smokers switching to opium. The Harrison Narcotics Act of 1914 made it illegal in the United States to sell or use opium, morphine, or cocaine. As a result many opium addicts switched to the more highly addictive heroin, which was not covered by the act. Crack cocaine, introduced as a cheaper alternative to regular cocaine in the 1980s, partly in response to the increases in street prices brought about by the War on Drugs, "is probably the most effective reinforcer of all available drugs" [says N.R. Carlson]. The search for possible legal substitutes for various psychotropic drugs led to the introduction of so-called designer drugs. In 1992 a contaminated batch of these designer drugs resulted in several individuals developing the symptoms of severe Parkinson's disease—the victims froze up and could not talk or move. And in the second half of the

19th century, high taxes on whisky in the United States led many individuals to substitute opium and hashish. Obviously, attempts to regulate along one margin simply lead to a shift to another, and often the substitute product is a more highly concentrated form than the one it replaced and thus potentially more harmful. Furthermore, a potential effect of the consumption of substances with higher concentration levels of their active ingredient will be a higher set point than would otherwise be the case, and, as a result, regulation may increase the average severity of the addiction problem for users of potentially addictive substances.

In sum, prohibition results in substitutions along several margins, most of which, when coupled with biology effects, work in the opposite direction of the goal of reducing harmful outcomes. Prohibition has adverse effects that complicate the addiction problem. By increasing concentrations, it increases the reinforcing strength of substances and thus is more likely to lead to naïve users quickly becoming addicted and increase the severity of the addiction resulting from increasing the set point. Also, variations in the quality and concentration increase the difficulty of the learning problem faced by naive users—for example, unanticipated variations in concentration can lead to fatal overdoses.

"[Efforts to prevent alcohol-related problems must] include public policy changes that would include . . . regulating the advertising."

Regulating Alcohol Advertising Will Reduce Alcohol Abuse

Jean Kilbourne

To prevent the problems associated with alcohol abuse, alcohol advertising must be regulated, argues Jean Kilbourne in the following viewpoint. In order to appeal to their best customers—alcoholics—beverage companies promote alcohol abuse by creating myths that alcohol improves life when in fact alcohol addiction destroys lives, she contends. The alcohol industry, Kilbourne maintains, should not be allowed to make alcohol use appear harmless because such myth-making impedes efforts to educate the public about the real dangers of alcohol abuse. Jean Kilbourne, EdD, is the author of *Can't Buy My Love: How Advertising Changes the Way We Think and Feel* (Simon & Schuster, 2000) and the creator of several award-winning films, including the "Killing Us Softly: Advertising's Image of Women" series.

As you read, consider the following questions:
1. According to Kilbourne, what would happen to the alcohol industry's gross revenue if alcoholics were to stop drinking?
2. Why is the college market particularly important to the alcohol industry, in the author's view?
3. In Kilbourne's opinion, what is at the heart of the alcoholic's dilemma and denial?

Jean Kilbourne, "Targets of Alcohol Advertising," *Health 20-20*, 2000. Copyright © 2000 by *Health 20-20*. Reproduced by permission of the author.

A lcohol is the most commonly used drug in the United States. It is also one of the most heavily advertised products in the United States. The alcohol industry generates more than $65 billion a year in revenue and spends more than $3 billion on advertising. The advertising budget for one beer—Budweiser—is more than the entire federal budget for research on alcoholism and alcohol use. Unfortunately, young people and heavy drinkers are the primary targets of the advertisers.

There is no conclusive proof that advertising increases alcohol consumption. The research is clear that, in addition to parents and peers, alcohol advertising and marketing have a significant impact on youth decisions to drink.

The alcohol industry claims that it is not trying to create more or heavier drinkers. It says that it only wants people who already drink to switch to another brand and that they want them to drink the new brand in moderation. But this industry-wide claim does not hold up under scrutiny. An editorial in *Advertising Age* concluded: "A strange world it is, in which people spending millions on advertising must do their best to prove that advertising doesn't do very much!"

About a third of Americans choose not to drink at all, a third drink moderately, and about a third drink regularly. Ten percent of the drinking-age population consumes over 60 percent of the alcohol. This figure corresponds closely to the percentage of alcoholics in society. If alcoholics were to recover (i.e., to stop drinking entirely), the alcohol industry's gross revenues would be cut in half.

Who Are the Industry's Targets?

Recognizing this important marketing fact, the alcohol industry deliberately devises ads designed to appeal to heavy drinkers. Most advertising is directed toward promoting brand loyalty and increasing usage. Obviously, the heavy users of any product are the best customers. However, when the product is a drug, the heavy user is often an addict. And any time an addict recovers, someone loses money, whether it is the pusher on the corner or the pusher in the boardroom.

If every adult in America drank according to the federal guidelines of what is low-risk drinking (which is no more than two drinks a day for a man and no more than one drink a day for a woman), alcohol industry sales would be cut by 80%. Although the alcohol companies claim they want people to drink "responsibly," the truth is that "responsible" drinking would destroy them.

These statistics show how important the heavy drinker is to the alcohol industry. Modern research techniques allow the producers of print and electronic media to provide advertisers with detailed information about their readers, listeners, and viewers. Target audiences are sold to the alcohol industry on a cost per drinker basis.

One example of how magazines sell target audiences appeared in *Advertising Age*, the major publication of the advertising industry. *Good Housekeeping* advertised itself to the alcohol industry as a good place to reach women drinkers, proclaiming "You'll catch more women with wine than with vinegar. She's a tougher customer than ever. You never needed *Good Housekeeping* more."

The Youth Market

The young audience is also worth a great deal to the alcohol industry. *Sport* magazine promoted itself to the alcohol industry as a conduit to young drinkers with an ad in *Advertising Age* stating, "What young money spends on drinks is a real eye-opener."

Social learning theory suggests that repeated exposure to modeled behavior can result in behavioral change. The impact of modeling on young people is particularly important given the widespread use of such celebrities as rock stars, television personalities, and athletes in alcohol ads. Alcohol ads feature only very healthy, attractive, and youthful-looking people. Advertising is a powerful educational force in American culture, one that promotes attitudes and values as well as products.

The "Seventh Special Report to the US Congress on Alcohol and Health" found evidence that early positive expectations about alcohol were strong predictors of drinking behavior in adolescence. "Children at highest risk were most likely to have strong expectancies of social enhancement and to believe that alcohol improves cognitive and motor functioning."

The Ad Campaigns

What more powerful source of these early expectancies is there in a culture than alcohol advertising? Indeed, one of the functions of advertising is to induce these early expectancies. According to an editorial in *Advertising Age*, "Quite clearly, the company that has not bothered to create a favorable attitude toward its product before the potential customer goes shopping hasn't much of a chance of snaring the bulk of potential buyers."

No wonder ads feature characters with special appeal to children. The Spuds MacKenzie [dog] . . . reportedly has been licensed by Anheuser-Busch to the makers of some 200 consumer products, including stuffed animals, dolls, T-shirts, posters, and mugs. In one Christmas ad campaign, Spuds appeared in a Santa Claus suit, promoting 12-packs of Bud Light beer. In another ad he is cavorting with ninjas, drawing on the popularity of the Teenage Mutant Ninja Turtles movie. "Heavy Metal," proclaims one Budweiser ad featuring a six-pack hardly an ad designed for the middle-aged crowd.

Many alcohol ads play on the theme that drinking is the primary ritual into adulthood in our society. Others turn soft drinks into alcoholic drinks, often in a way that scoffs at the idea of a soft drink standing alone (e.g., an ad for a wine cooler says, "Sick of soft drinks? Here's thirst aid.") In 2001 the alcohol industry introduced 130 new spirits, 46 new beers, and 103 new wines. Many of these were sweet products clearly designed to appeal to new drinkers, i.e. young people. These included chocolate and raspberry beer, gelatin shots, hard cider, hard lemonade, liquor popsicles, and drinks with alcohol premixed with milk, cola, jello, and ice cream.

Recent studies have found that alcohol ads are far more likely to appear in youth-oriented magazines and radio programs than in those aimed at adults. As a result, young people see more ads for beer than for jeans, sneakers, or gum. In addition, many films, especially those appealing to young people, include paid placements of cigarettes and alcohol.

The average age at which people begin drinking is 13. The most recent federal survey of school children found that 16.6% of eighth graders reported having been drunk at least once in the past year. By the tenth grade, that number is almost 40%. Children who begin drinking before the age of 15 are four times more likely to develop alcohol dependence than those who wait until the age of 21. Recent evidence indicates that alcohol damages the brains of young people and that the damage may be irreversible.

Youthful drinking is frequently characterized by high-risk heavy drinking, making youngsters a lucrative market for alcohol producers. Underage drinkers account for 12% of all alcohol sales. The most widely used illegal drug in America by far is beer. Junior and senior high school students alone drink over a billion cans of beer a year, spending almost $500 million.

The college market is particularly important to the alcohol industry not only because of the money the students will spend on beer today, but because they may develop drinking habits and brand allegiances for a lifetime. As one marketing executive said, "Let's not forget that getting a freshman to choose a certain brand of beer may mean that he will maintain his brand loyalty for the next 20 to 35 years. If he turns out to be a big drinker, the beer company has bought itself an annuity." This statement undercuts the industry's claim that it does not target advertising campaigns at underage drinkers since today almost every state prohibits the sale of alcohol to people under 21 years old and the vast majority of college freshmen are below that age. . . .

Creating Myths About Alcohol Use

Advertising does not cause alcoholism. Alcoholism is a complex illness and its etiology is uncertain. But alcohol advertising does create a climate in which abusive attitudes toward alcohol are presented as normal, appropriate, and innocuous. One of the chief symptoms of alcoholism is denial that there is a problem. It is often not only the alcoholic who denies the illness but also his or her family, employer, doctor, etc. Alcohol advertising often encourages denial by creating a world in which myths about alcohol are presented as true and in which signs of trouble are erased or transformed into positive attributes.

One of the primary means of creating this distortion is through advertising. Most advertising is essentially myth-making. Instead of providing information about a product, such as its taste or quality, advertisements create an image of the product, linking the item with a particular lifestyle which may have little or nothing to do with the product itself. According to an article on beer marketing in *Advertising Age*, "Advertising is as important to selling beer as the bottle opener is to drinking it. . . . Beer advertising is mainly an exercise in building images." Another article a few months later on liquor marketing stated that "product image is probably the most important element in selling liquor. The trick for marketers is to project the right message in their advertisements to motivate those motionless consumers to march down to the liquor store or bar and exchange their money for a sip of image."

The Normalization of Alcohol Use

The AMA [American Medical Association] long has focused on how alcohol advertising affects young people, who, studies show, typically will see 100,000 beer commercials before reaching age 18. These ads are a major contributor to the "normalization" of alcohol use by children and youth—a phenomenon that has reached epidemic proportions. About 11 million Americans younger than 21 drink, and nearly half of them drink to excess. Boys usually try alcohol for the first time at just 11 years old, while the average first-drink age for American girls is 13.

American Medical Association, Amednews.com, February 24, 2003.

The links are generally false and arbitrary but we are so surrounded by them that we come to accept them: the jeans will make you look sexy, the car will give you confidence, the detergent will save your marriage.

Advertising spuriously links alcohol with precisely those attributes and qualities such as happiness, wealth, prestige, sophistication, success, maturity, athletic ability, virility, creativity, sexual satisfaction, and others, that the use of alcohol destroys. For example, alcohol is often linked with romance and sexual fulfillment, yet it is common knowledge that alcohol use can lead to sexual dysfunction. Less well known is the fact that heavy drinkers and alcoholics are seven times more likely than the general population to be separated or divorced.

Image advertising is especially appealing to young people who are more likely than adults to be insecure about the image they are projecting. Sexual and athletic prowess are two of the themes that dominate advertising aimed at young people. A television commercial for Miller beer featured Danny Sullivan, the race car driver, speeding around a track with the Miller logo emblazoned everywhere. The ad implies that Miller beer and fast driving go hand in hand. A study of beer commercials funded by the American Automobile Association found that they often linked beer with images of speed, including speeding cars.

"It separates the exceptional from the merely ordinary." This advertising slogan for Piper champagne illustrates the major premise of the mythology that alcohol is magic. It is a magic potion that can make you successful, sophisticated, and sexy; without it you are dull, mediocre, and ordinary. The people who are not drinking champagne are lifeless replicas of the happy couple who are imbibing. The alcohol has rescued the couple, resurrected them, restored them to life. At the heart of the alcoholic's dilemma and denial is this belief, this certainty, that alcohol is essential for life, that without it he or she will literally die or at least suffer. This ad and many others like it present the nightmare as true, thus affirming and even glorifying one of the symptoms of the illness.

Distorting the Dangers

Such glorification of the symptoms is common in alcohol advertising. "Your own special island," proclaims an ad for St. Croix rum. Another ad offers Busch beer as "Your mountain hide-a-way." Almost all alcoholics experience intense feelings of isolation, alienation, and loneliness. Most make the tragic mistake of believing that alcohol alleviates these feelings rather than exacerbates them. The two examples above distort reality in much the same way the alcoholic does. Instead of being isolated and alienated, the people in the ad are in their own special places.

The rum ad also seems to be encouraging solitary drinking, a sign of trouble with alcohol. There is one drink on the tray and no room for another. Although it is unusual for solitary drinking to be shown (most alcohol ads feature groups or happy couples), it is not unusual for unhealthful attitudes toward alcohol to be presented as normal and acceptable.

The most obvious example is obsession with alcohol. Alcohol is at the center of the ads just as it is at the center of the alcoholic's life. The ads imply that alcohol is an appropriate adjunct to almost every activity from love-making to white-water canoeing. An ad for Puerto Rican rums says, "You know how to make every day special. You're a white rum drinker." In fact, less than 10 percent of the adult population makes drinking a part of their daily routine.

There is also an emphasis on quantity in the ads. A Johnnie Walker ad features 16 bottles of scotch and the copy, "Bob really knows how to throw a party. He never runs out of Johnnie Walker Red." Light beer has been developed and heavily promoted not for the dieter but for the heavy drinker. The ads imply that because it is less filling, one can drink more of it.

Thus the ads tell the alcoholic and everyone around him that it is all right to consume large quantities of alcohol on a daily basis and to have it be a part of all of one's activities. At the same time, all signs of trouble and any hint of addiction are conspicuously avoided. The daily drinking takes place in glorious and unique settings, such as yachts at sunset, not at the more mundane but realistic kitchen tables in the morning. There is no unpleasant drunkenness, only high spirits. There are never any negative consequences. Of course, one would not expect there to be. The advertisers are selling their product and it is their job to erase any negative aspects as well as to enhance the positive ones. When the product is a drug that is addictive to one out of ten users, however, some consequences go far beyond product sales.

Western culture as a whole, not just the advertising and alcohol industry, tends to glorify alcohol and dismiss the problems associated with it. The "war on drugs," as covered by newspapers and magazines in this country, rarely includes the two major killers, alcohol and nicotine. It is no coincidence that these are two of the most heavily advertised products. The use of all illicit drugs combined accounts for about 14,000 deaths a year. Alcohol is linked with over 100,000 deaths annually. Cigarettes kill a thousand people every day.

A comprehensive public health effort is needed to prevent alcohol-related problems. Such an effort must include education, media campaigns, increased availability of treatment programs and more effective deterrence policies. It must also include public policy changes that would include raising taxes on alcohol, putting clearly legible warning labels on the bottles, and regulating the advertising.

The kind of public education essential to solving our major drug problem is probably not possible until the media no longer depend on the goodwill of the alcohol industry. For this reason alone, we need some controls on alcohol. One doesn't even have to enter into the argument about whether such advertising increases consumption. At the very least, it drastically inhibits honest public discussion of the problem in the media and creates a climate in which alcohol use is seen as entirely benign.

"Restrictions on [alcohol] advertising will not reduce or eliminate misuse."

Regulating Alcohol Advertising Will Not Reduce Alcohol Abuse

Advertising Association

In the following viewpoint the Advertising Association, a federation of trade bodies representing advertising and promotional marketing industries in Great Britain, argues that restrictions on alcohol advertising will not reduce alcohol abuse. The association claims that no studies have established a causal connection between alcohol advertising and increased consumption. In fact, the association maintains, countries that have imposed bans have actually seen an increase in teen alcohol consumption. According to the association, alcohol advertising is not designed to increase overall consumption but to encourage consumers to switch brands.

As you read, consider the following questions:
1. In the Advertising Association's view, what are some of the causal factors related to alcohol abuse?
2. What had been happening to alcohol consumption in France before the implementation of the Loi Evin in 1991, according to the author?
3. How are organizations that portray restrictions on advertising as a panacea for the problems associated with alcohol mistaken, in the association's opinion?

Advertising Association, "Alcohol Advertising," www.adassoc.org.uk, December 2000. Copyright © 2000 by The Advertising Association. Reproduced by permission.

In spite of the proven success of advertising regulation and the responsible attitude of the advertising industry, there is criticism about alcohol advertising, especially in relation to its presumed impact on consumption and abusive consumption. Such criticism is, more often than not, based on a lack of understanding about the role of advertising and confusion between "brand advertising" and "generic advertising".

In general, companies advertise their own brands in order to increase the overall market share of their brands alone and to protect that market share against brand switching by consumers. Brand advertising, of the type seen in the alcoholic drinks market sector, is a tool of competition between brands, not a means to ensure overall increases in total consumption of a product type.

Moreover, there is no relationship between responsible brand advertising in the alcoholic drinks sector and the misuse of the product itself. The causal factors related to alcohol abuse are many. They include social, economic, demographic and perhaps genetic influences upon which brand advertising has little or no impact. Restrictions on advertising will not reduce or eliminate misuse as the experience of countries in which bans have been imposed shows. According to a paper entitled "The Drinking Revolution: Building a Campaign for Safer Drinking", published by Alcohol Concern in 1987: "There is little or no evidence that advertising increases total consumption of alcohol as against increasing a particular product's share of the market."

Per capita consumption of alcohol is lower today in Europe than it has been for most of the past three centuries. In addition, the UK [United Kingdom] actually has lower rates of "officially recorded" consumption than almost any ether country in Western Europe, other than the Scandinavian countries and Iceland, where high taxes and national alcohol policies have led to very high levels of unrecorded consumption. France, where an ad ban has been in place since 1991, continues to have a very high level of alcohol consumption and is in second place in the Western Europe per capita alcohol consumption league.

The US Federal Trade Commission's (FTC) Bureaux of Consumer Protection & Economics undertook a review of the available literature on alcohol advertising and consumption in 1985. This extensive government survey of the literature concerning the general effects of advertising reached conclusions that were further confirmed by similar FTC appraisals directed specifically at the alcoholic drinks sector. The review of evidence concluded that: "The large majority of such studies found little or no effect of advertising on total industry demand."

Reviewing the Studies

A study by [B.] Chiplin, [B.] Sturgess and [J.H.] Dunning in 1981 also concluded that: "It remains unproven that advertising has led to any marked increase in aggregate demand in general, or in the demand for . . . alcohol . . . It must be recognised that advertising could well be the wrong target in seeking to curtail consumption of products such as . . . alcohol. . . . It does appear that so far there is little convincing support for the argument that changes in total consumption of these products are caused by advertising."

A more recent independent review of the available literature carried out by [J.E.] Calfee and [C.] Scheraga in 1989 concluded that: "Econometric and laboratory research in the US, Canada and the UK have not revealed advertising to have a significant effect on alcohol consumption. The same is true of survey research which confirms the powerful role of social factors such as the attitudes and behaviour of parents and peers."

The authors go on to say that: "The data shows that social forces other than prices and income were bringing about a strong reduction in demand for alcoholic beverages and that advertising did nothing to ward off this trend."

One study, published in 1981, has been quoted by many observers as demonstrating a link between advertising and consumption. This study was [C.] Atkin & [M.] Block: "Content and Effects of Alcohol Advertising", National Technical Information Service (USA) 1981. However, in April 1992, Dr Block submitted evidence to a US Senate Subcommittee which included the following reference to his 1981 study: "This study does not demonstrate that exposure to alcohol advertising causes consumption of alcohol that would not otherwise occur. . . . Most importantly, from my review of the scientific literature, I can find no persuasive evidence that advertising causes non-drinkers to start drinking or that advertising causes drinkers to become abusers . . . if anything the advertisements we studied would reinforce only moderate consumption. . . ."

Although these remarks referred to the findings of Dr Block from US sources, many of the ads described were produced by advertisers and agencies who market and advertise the same or similar brands in Europe and follow similar self-regulatory codes.

The French Connection

Many organizations calling for tighter restrictions on alcoholic drinks advertising cite the example of France as providing substantiation for their arguments.

Per capita alcohol consumption in France had peaked during the mid 1950s. The decline that followed was halted briefly in the early 1970s only to resume even more strongly in the later part of that decade. It should be noted that in spite of this decline, France continues to have one of the highest rates of alcohol consumption in Europe. At first these reductions in French consumption were driven by the increased availability of clean drinking water. Then changing lifestyles took over. Adults began to drop the habit of drinking liqueurs after dinner. Younger consumers gradually abandoned the traditional French preference for wine with every meal and adopted the more international preference for beer, soft drinks and "lighter products" generally.

In 1991 the French Government implemented the Loi Evin with the explicit purpose of reducing the health costs of alcohol abuse. The law severely restricts alcoholic drinks advertising.

The downward slide in consumption continued through 1994 virtually as it had in the fifteen years before the Loi Evin was enacted, despite the fact that advertising declined precipitously after the law was passed.

In 1997, John E Calfee (Resident Scholar at the American Enterprise Institute for Public Policy Research, Washington DC) revisited the issue of advertising and consumption in his book entitled "Fear of Persuasion: A New Perspective on Advertising and Regulation". Calfee examined the situation within France and concluded that: "Statistical analysis confirmed that advertising has had no discernible effect in increasing French total alcohol consumption above what it would otherwise have been. Of course market shares have shifted (wine's share has fallen dramatically for example) and advertising is presumably a factor in those shifts. But advertising has had no detectable effect in the deeper issue of how much drinking occurs overall."

Should the Government Restrict Advertising of Alcoholic Beverages?

As a psychiatrist, scientist, and former architect of the national effort to prevent alcohol problems, it was my job to seek out the best science, both biomedical and behavioral. Today, a heated debate swirls around the issue of restricting alcohol advertising on TV. Assorted opponents who argue that advertising contributes to alcohol-related problems—especially among young people—are way off base.

When I consider the pros and cons of alcohol advertising and its alleged effect on problem drinking, I find myself asking the crucial question: Where in the name of science is there proof that alcohol advertising is bad for society? Shouldn't there be some science to say it's so?

[In 1996] I was asked to write a review for the *New England Journal of Medicine* on how advertising affects alcohol use. I did not find *any* studies that credibly connect advertising to increases in alcohol use (or abuse) or to young persons taking up drinking.

Morris E. Chafetz, *Priorities*, 1997.

More recently, a new survey of alcohol consumption in France by the French Health Education Authority has found that French teenagers are actually smoking and drinking more per year since 1991, the year in which the ban on alcohol and tobacco advertising was introduced. Furthermore, since the imposition of the Loi Evin, a competitive new market for low priced high strength own label beer has emerged. This category (now sold in supermarkets and apparently drunk by those "seeking inebriation") increased by no less than 33% between 1991 and 1996. Over the same period, alcohol consumption by teenagers has actually increased—the opposite of what was intended. . . .

Current Regulation Is Enough

Independent, academic research based on statistical evidence and taking into account prices, incomes, sales and ad-spend illustrates that, at most, advertising has a statistically insignificant effect on consumption. There is little or no overall impact on total category consumption as a result of brand advertising. This would reinforce the argument put forward by the advertising industry that in a mature market such as alcoholic drinks, advertising is targeted to reinforce brand identity, offset brand-switching and maintain market share rather than encourage greater levels of overall consumption across the category.

Evidence from countries in which advertising bans have been imposed show that, contrary to the arguments put forward by some lobbying organizations, these bans have little or no effect on reducing consumption, particularly among target groups such as young people.

The current regulatory structures in the UK are working well and are regularly reviewed to take into account perceived problems and changes in public opinion. Responsible advertising is the norm in the alcoholic drinks sector and compliance with existing regulations is high.

Those organizations that continue to portray restrictions on advertising as a panacea for the problems associated with alcohol misuse, whilst undoubtedly well-intentioned, are mistaken in their belief that restricting legitimate freedom of speech is a credible addition or alternative to a logical anti-misuse strategy.

Periodical Bibliography

The following articles have been selected to supplement the diverse views presented in this chapter.

Richard Amberg	"Addicted to Lotteries," *Insight*, September 20, 1999.
Tom Bell	"Internet Gambling: Impossible to Stop, Wrong to Outlaw," *Regulation*, Winter 1998.
Joseph A. Califano	"It's All in the Family," *America*, January 15, 2000.
Guy Calvert	"Gambling and the Good Society," *World & I*, July 2000.
Mary H. Cooper	"Drug Policy Debate," *CQ Researcher*, July 28, 2000.
Thomas A. Hemphill	"Harmonizing Alcohol Ads: Another Case for Industry Self-Regulation," *Regulation*, Spring 1998.
Robert Higgs	"We're All Sick, and Government Must Heal Us," *Independent Review*, Spring 1999.
Michael deCourcy Hinds	"Gambling: Is It a Problem? What Should We Do?" *National Issues Forums*, 1998.
James Kilpatrick	"Gambling Is Bad, but Freedom Is Good," *Conservative Chronicle*, January 13, 1999.
Joe Loconte	"Killing Them Softly," *Policy Review*, July/August 1998.
Davis Masci	"Preventing Teen Drug Use," *CQ Researcher*, March 15, 2002.
William D. McColl	"The Politics of Drug Issues," *Counselor*, October 2000.
Max Pappas	"Betting on IT," *Foreign Policy*, July/August 2003.
Bill Stronach	"Alcohol Advertising Must Be Curtailed to Change Attitudes to Drinking," *Online Opinion*, July 3, 2003.
Eric A. Voth	"America's Longest 'War,'" *World & I*, February 2000.

For Further Discussion

Chapter 1

1. Brian McCormick claims that the Internet has made it easier for addicts to act out their compulsive behaviors. Jacob Sullum agrees that the Internet can lead to compulsive behaviors but argues that the Internet is not like a drug; therefore, he asserts, making comparisons between compulsive Internet activity and excessive drug use leads to an exaggeration of the problems associated with Internet use. How does each author view the nature of addiction? How is this reflected in their arguments? Explain, citing from the viewpoints.

2. The National Institute on Drug Abuse argues that nicotine is a highly addictive substance. Dale M. Atrens claims that this assumption—that nicotine is addictive—is widespread, yet it is not supported by research. Does Atrens's analysis of the research convince you that nicotine is not addictive? Why or why not?

3. Tom Grey claims that compulsive gambling is a serious problem. Steve Chapman maintains that opposition to gambling is based on faulty assumptions. What evidence do the authors use to support their views? Based on their use of evidence, whose argument do you find more persuasive and why?

Chapter 2

1. Alan I. Leshner argues that addiction is a disease that should be treated as a medical problem. Jeffrey A. Schaler claims that addiction is a voluntary behavior that should not be treated like a medical problem. To support his view, Schaler contends that research showing that drug and alcohol use generates electrochemical changes in the brain does not prove that future drug use is therefore involuntary. Is the failure to prove a direct connection between electrochemical changes and future drug use sufficient to convince you that addiction should not be treated as a medical problem? Explain why or why not.

2. Kenneth M. Sunamoto cites research to support his view that marijuana leads to the use of other illicit drugs. Mitch Earleywine also cites evidence to support his argument that marijuana does not lead to the use of other illicit drugs. Which author's use of evidence do you find more persuasive? Explain, citing from the text.

3. Ernest P. Noble argues that understanding the gene that predisposes some people to drug addiction may lead to more effective

addiction treatments. Judy Shepps Battle agrees that genetics play a part in drug addiction, but she claims that environmental factors should be addressed in order to prevent and treat addiction. Which approach do you think would be more effective to treat addiction? Explain, citing from the viewpoints.

Chapter 3

1. Krista Conger maintains that twelve-step programs are more likely to lead to abstinence than are cognitive-behavioral programs that teach coping skills. Maia Szalavitz does not dispute that twelve-step programs are effective for some people, but she argues that the treatment community's emphasis on these programs discourages those who might require more medically based treatment options. Based on the evidence these authors provide, do you think health care practitioners should emphasize twelve-step programs at the exclusion of other treatments? Explain, citing from the texts.

2. Do you agree with Kevin Courcey's assessment of the study conducted by the National Center on Addiction and Substance Abuse? Why or why not?

3. Sharon Stancliff argues that methadone is an effective treatment for heroin addiction. I.E. Hawksworth claims that heroin addicts abuse methadone programs and recommends different treatment strategies. Stancliff is a physician and director of a methadone maintenance treatment program while Hawksworth is a former addict. How does knowing the authors' backgrounds affect your evaluation of their arguments?

4. Sally L. Satel and Mike Harden use different terms to define people who have problems with alcohol. How does the way each author describes these people differ? How do the differences reflect their respective stances on the merits of moderation?

Chapter 4

1. Richard Blumenthal sees the Internet gambling industry as an unsavory business that takes advantage of vulnerable addicts. Fred E. Foldvary, on the other hand, sees the industry as a traditional business trying to compete for the dollars of willing consumers. How is the way these authors view the Internet gambling industry reflected in their viewpoints?

2. In defense of laws prohibiting use of illegal drugs, John P. Walters argues that drugs, not the laws that prohibit them, hurt addicts, their families, and society. Adam Gifford argues that when governments try to regulate drugs, addicts simply adapt their

behavior to maintain their addiction or shift to other, possibly more dangerous, substances. Based on the evidence these authors provide, do you think prohibition of drugs protects or harms addicts? Explain, citing from the texts.

3. Jean Kilbourne argues that alcohol advertising should be regulated because it misleads alcoholics—the alcohol industry's best customers—into believing that alcohol is a benign substance that makes life better, when in fact, alcohol can be deadly. The Advertising Association argues that no causal connection has been established between increased alcohol consumption and alcohol advertising. Do you agree that in order to justify the regulation of alcohol advertising a causal connection between alcohol ads and increased consumption must be proven? Explain.

Organizations to Contact

The editors have compiled the following list of organizations concerned with the issues debated in this book. The descriptions are derived from materials provided by the organizations. All have publications or information available for interested readers. The list was compiled on the date of publication of the present volume; names, addresses, phone and fax numbers, and e-mail and Internet addresses may change. Be aware that many organizations take several weeks or longer to respond to inquiries, so allow as much time as possible.

Addiction Resource Guide
PO Box 8612, Tarrytown, NY 10591
(914) 725-5151 • fax: (914) 631-8077
e-mail: info@addictionresourceguide.com
website: www.addictionresourceguide.com

The Addiction Resource Guide is a comprehensive online directory of addiction treatment facilities, programs, and resources. The Inpatient Treatment Facility directory provides in-depth profiles of treatment facilities. The resources directory is a comprehensive listing of links for laypeople and professionals.

Alcoholics Anonymous (AA)
Grand Central Station, PO Box 459, New York, NY 10163
(212) 870-3400 • fax: (212) 870-3003
website: www.aa.org

Alcoholics Anonymous is a worldwide fellowship of sober alcoholics, whose recovery is based on twelve steps. AA requires no dues or fees and accepts no outside funds. It is self-supporting through voluntary contributions of members and is not affiliated with any other organization. AA's primary purpose is to carry the AA message to the alcoholic. Its publications include the book *Alcoholics Anonymous* (more commonly known as the Big Book) and the pamphlets *A Brief Guide to Alcoholics Anonymous, Young People and AA*, and *AA Traditions—How It Developed*.

American Council on Science and Health (ACSH)
1995 Broadway, 2nd Fl., New York, NY 10023-5860
(212) 362-7044 • fax: (212) 362-4919
e-mail: acsh@acsh.org • website: www.acsh.org

ACSH is a consumer education group concerned with issues related to food, nutrition, chemicals, pharmaceuticals, lifestyle, the environment, and health. It publishes the quarterly newsletter *Pri-*

orities as well as the booklets *The Tobacco Industry's Use of Nicotine as a Drug* and *A Comparison of the Health Effects of Alcohol Consumption and Tobacco Use in America.*

Canadian Centre on Substance Abuse (CCSA)
75 Albert St., Suite 300, Ottawa, ON K1P 5E7 Canada
(613) 235-4048 • fax: (613) 235-8101
e-mail: info@ccsa.ca • website: www.ccsa.ca

Established in 1988 by an act of Parliament, the CCSA works to minimize the harm associated with the use of alcohol, tobacco, and other drugs by sponsoring public debates on this issue. It disseminates information on the nature, extent, and consequences of substance abuse and supports organizations involved in substance abuse treatment, prevention, and educational programming. The center publishes the newsletter *Action News* six times a year.

Canadian Foundation for Drug Policy (CFDP)
70 MacDonald St., Ottawa, ON K2P 1H6 Canada
(613) 236-1027 • fax: (613) 238-2891
e-mail: eoscapel@fox.nstn.ca • website: www.cfdp.ca

Founded by several of Canada's leading drug policy specialists, the CFDP examines the objectives and consequences of Canada's drug laws and policies. When necessary, the foundation recommends alternatives that it believes would make Canada's drug policies more effective and humane. The CFDP also disseminates educational material.

Canadian Foundation on Compulsive Gambling (CFCG)
Responsible Gambling Council
505 Consumers Rd., Suite 801, Toronto, ON M2J 4V8 Canada
(416) 499-9800 • 1-888-391-1111 • fax: (416) 499-8260
e-mail: infosource@cfcg.org • website: www.cfcg.org

CFCG conducts research into compulsive gambling and supports public awareness programs designed to prevent gambling-related problems. On its website, the CFCG provides a library of articles and research reports, links to treatment resources, and recent news about gambling issues.

Drug Enforcement Administration (DEA)
2401 Jefferson Davis Hwy., Arlington, VA 22301
website: www.usdoj.gov/dea

The DEA is the federal agency charged with enforcing the nation's drug laws. The agency concentrates on stopping the smuggling and distribution of narcotics in the United States and abroad. It publishes the *Drug Enforcement Magazine* three times a year.

The Lindesmith Center–Drug Policy Foundation (TLC-DPF)
4455 Connecticut Ave. NW, Suite B-500, Washington, DC 20008-2328
(202) 537-5005 • fax: (202) 537-3007
e-mail: information@drugpolicy.org
website: www.lindesmith.org

The Lindesmith Center–Drug Policy Foundation seeks to educate Americans and others about alternatives to current drug policies on issues including adolescent drug use, policing drug markets, and alternatives to incarceration. TLC-DPF also addresses issues of drug policy reform through a variety of projects, including the International Harm Reduction Development (IHRD), a response to increased drug use and HIV transmissions in eastern Europe. The center also publishes fact sheets on topics such as needle and syringe availability and drug education.

Moderation Management (MM)
c/o HRC, 22 W. 27th St., New York, NY 10001
(212) 871-0974 • fax: (212) 213-6582
e-mail: mm@moderation.org • website: www.moderation.org

Moderation Management is a recovery program and national support group for people who have made the decision to reduce their drinking and make other positive lifestyle changes. MM empowers individuals to accept personal responsibility for choosing and maintaining their own recovery path, whether moderation or abstinence. It offers the book *Responsible Drinking, A Moderation Management Approach for Problem Drinkers*, as well as other suggested reading material, including books, pamphlets, and guidelines regarding drinking in moderation.

Narcotics Anonymous (NA)
World Services Office, PO Box 9999, Van Nuys, CA 91409
(818) 773-9999 • fax: (818) 700-0700

Narcotics Anonymous, comprising more than eighteen thousand groups worldwide, is an organization of recovering drug addicts who meet regularly to help each other abstain from drugs. It publishes the monthly *NA Way Magazine* and annual conference reports.

National Center on Addiction and Substance Abuse at Columbia University (CASA)
633 3rd Ave., 19th Floor, New York, NY 10017-6706
(212) 841-5200
website: www.casacolumbia.org

CASA is a private, nonprofit organization that works to educate the public about the hazards of chemical dependency. The organization supports treatment as the best way to reduce chemical dependency. It produces publications describing the harmful effects of alcohol and drug addiction and effective ways to address the problem of substance abuse. Its reports include the "National Survey of American Attitudes on Substance Abuse," "Research on Drug Courts," and "So Help Me God: Substance Abuse, Religion and Spirituality."

National Coalition Against Legalized Gambling (NCALG)
110 Maryland Ave. NE, Room 311, Washington, DC 20002
(800) 664-2680 • (307) 587-8082
e-mail: ncalg@ncalg.org • website: www.ncalg.org

NCALG is an antigambling organization that seeks to educate the public, policy makers, and media about the social and economic costs of gambling. On its website, NCALG provides news of recent legislation and current and archived issues of the NCALG quarterly newsletter.

National Council on Alcoholism and Drug Dependence (NCADD)
20 Exchange Pl., Suite 2902, New York, NY 10005
(212) 269-7797 • fax: (212) 269-7510
e-mail: national@ncadd.org • website: www.ncadd.org

NCADD is a volunteer health organization that helps individuals overcome addictions, develops substance abuse prevention and education programs for youth, and advises the federal government on drug and alcohol policies. It operates the Campaign to Prevent Kids from Drinking. Publications include brochures and fact sheets such as "Youth, Alcohol and Other Drugs."

National Council on Sexual Addiction and Compulsivity (NCSAC)
PO Box 725544, Atlanta, GA 31139
(770) 541-9912 • (770) 541-1566
e-mail: ncsac@mindspring.com • website: www.ncsac.org

The goal of the NCSAC is to promote acceptance of the diagnosis of sexual addiction and sexual compulsivity. NCSAC provides up-to-date research and information on sexual addiction for addicts and professionals who work with people struggling with sexual addiction and compulsion. Publications include *Sexual Addiction and Compulsivity: The Journal of Treatment and Prevention* and the *NCSAC Newsletter*. Its website provides papers and articles on sexual addiction.

National Institute on Alcohol Abuse and Alcoholism (NIAAA)
Willco Building
6000 Executive Blvd., Bethesda, MD 20892-7003
(301) 496-4000
e-mail: niaaaweb-r@exchange.nih.gov
website: www.niaaa.nih.gov

NIAAA supports and conducts biomedical and behavioral research on the causes, consequences, treatment, and prevention of alcoholism and alcohol-related problems. The institute disseminates the findings of this research to the public, researchers, policy makers, and health care providers. The NIAAA publishes pamphlets, reports, the quarterly journal *Alcohol Research & Health* (formerly *Alcohol Health & Research World*), and *Alcohol Alert* bulletins.

National Institute on Drug Abuse (NIDA)
U.S. Department of Health and Human Services
6001 Executive Blvd., Room 5213, Bethesda, MD 20892
(301) 443-1124
e-mail: information@lists.nida.nih.gov
website: www.nida.nih.gov

NIDA supports and conducts research on drug abuse—including the yearly Monitoring the Future survey—in order to improve addiction prevention, treatment, and policy efforts. It publishes the bimonthly *NIDA Notes* newsletter and a catalog of research reports and public education materials.

Office of National Drug Control Policy (ONDCP)
Drug Policy Information Clearinghouse
PO Box 6000, Rockville, MD 20849-6000
(800) 666-3332 • fax: (301) 519-5212
e-mail: ondcp@ncjrs.org
website: www.whitehousedrugpolicy.gov

The Office of National Drug Control Policy formulates the government's national drug strategy and the president's antidrug policy and coordinates the federal agencies responsible for stopping drug trafficking. Its reports include "National Drug Control Strategy, 2002" and "Get It Straight! The Facts About Drugs."

Rational Recovery
Box 800, Lotus, CA 95651
(530) 621-2667
e-mail: icc@rational.org • website: www.rational.org/recovery

Rational Recovery is a national self-help organization that offers a cognitive rather than spiritual approach to recovery from alcoholism. Its philosophy holds that alcoholics can attain sobriety without depending on other people or a "higher power." It publishes materials including the bimonthly *Journal of Rational Recovery* and the book *Rational Recovery: The New Cure for Substance Addiction.*

Secular Organization for Sobriety (SOS)
SOS National Clearinghouse, The Center for Inquiry—West
4773 Hollywood Blvd., Hollywood, CA 90026
(323) 666-4295 • fax: (323) 666-4271
e-mail: sos@cfiwest.org
website: www.secularhumanism.org/sos

SOS is an alternative recovery method for alcoholics or drug addicts who are uncomfortable with the spiritual content of twelve-step programs. SOS takes a secular approach to recovery and maintains that sobriety is a separate issue from religion or spirituality. Its publications include the books *How to Stay Sober: Recovery Without Religion* and *Unhooked: Staying Sober and Drug Free* as well as the *SOS International Newsletter.*

Stanton Peele Addiction Website
website: www.peele.net

Stanton Peele has been investigating and writing about addiction since 1969. His approach to addiction revolutionized thinking on the subject by suggesting that addiction is not limited to narcotics and that addiction is a pattern of behavior that is best understood by examining an individual's relationship with his or her world. Peele is also a well-known opponent of the American medical model of treating alcohol and drug abuse. Peele has written numerous books and articles in support of his position, many of which are available on his website, including *The Nature of Addiction* and *The Politics and Persecution of Controlled Drinking and Drug Use.*

Bibliography of Books

Caroline Jean Acker — *Creating the American Junkie: Addiction Research in the Classic Era of Narcotic Control.* Baltimore: Johns Hopkins University Press, 2002.

Rachel Green Baldino — *Welcome to Methadonia: A Social Worker's Candid Account of Life in a Methadone Clinic.* Harrisburg, PA: White Hat Communications, 2001.

Terry Burnham — *Mean Genes: From Sex to Money to Food, Taming Our Primal Instincts.* Cambridge, MA: Perseus, 2000.

Patrick Carnes — *In the Shadows of the Net: Breaking Free of Compulsive Online Sexual Behavior.* Center City, MN: Hazeldon, 2001.

Rosalyn Carson-Dewitt and Joseph W. Weiss, eds. — *Drugs, Alcohol, and Tobacco: Learning About Addictive Behavior.* New York: MacMillan Reference Books, 2003.

Rod Colvin — *Prescription Drug Addiction: The Hidden Epidemic.* Omaha, NE: Addicus Books, 2001.

Al Cooper — *Cybersex: The Dark Side of the Force.* Philadelphia: Brunner-Routledge, 2000.

Carlo C. DiClemente — *Addiction and Change: How Addictions Develop and Addicted People Recover.* New York: Guilford Press, 2003.

Robert L. Dupont and Betty Ford — *The Selfish Brain: Learning from Addiction.* Washington, DC: Hazeldon Information Education, 2000.

Jon Elster and Ole-Jørgen Skog, eds. — *Getting Hooked: Rationality and Addiction.* New York: Cambridge University Press, 1999.

Stanley D. Glick and Isabelle M. Maisonneuve, eds. — *New Medications for Drug Abuse.* New York: New York Academy of Sciences, 2000.

Marcus Grant and Jorge Litvak, eds. — *Drinking Patterns and Their Consequences.* Washington, DC: Taylor & Francis, 1998.

Jonathan Gruber — *Is Addiction "Rational"?: Theory and Evidence.* Cambridge, MA: National Bureau of Economic Research, 2000.

Glen Hanson, Peter Venturelli, and Annette E. Fleckenstein, eds. — *Drugs and Society.* Boston: Jones and Bartlett, 2001.

Philip B. Heymann and William N. Brownsberger, eds. — *Drug Addiction and Drug Policy: The Struggle to Control Dependence.* Cambridge, MA: Harvard University Press, 2001.

James A. Inciardi and Lana D. Harrison, eds.
Harm Reduction: National and International Perspectives. Thousand Oaks, CA: Sage, 2000.

Denise B. Kandel, ed.
Stages and Pathways of Drug Involvement: Examining the Gateway Hypothesis. New York: Cambridge University Press, 2002.

Little Hoover Commission
For Our Health and Safety: Joining Forces to Defeat Addiction. Sacramento: Little Hoover Commissions, 2003.

David F. Musto
The American Disease: Origins of Narcotic Control. New York: Oxford University Press, 1999.

Stanton Peele
The Diseasing of America: How We Allowed Recovery Zealots and the Treatment Industry to Convince Us We Are Out of Control. San Francisco: Jossey-Bass, 1999.

Stanton Peele
The Meaning of Addiction: An Unconventional View. San Francisco: Jossey-Bass, 1998.

Jeffrey A. Schaler
Addiction Is a Choice. Chicago: Open Court, 2000.

Jennifer P. Schneider
Cybersex Exposed: Simple Fantasy or Obsession? Center City, MN: Hazeldon, 2001.

Paul Slovic, ed.
Smoking: Risk, Perception, and Policy. Thousand Oaks, CA: Sage, 2001.

Jacob Sullum
For Your Own Good: The Anti-Smoking Crusade and the Tyranny of Public Health. New York: Free Press, 1998.

Glenn D. Walters
Addiction Concept: Working Hypothesis or Self-Fulfilling Prophecy? New York: Pearson Higher Education, 1998.

Martin Weegmann and Robert Cohen, eds.
The Psychodynamics of Addiction. London: Whurr, 2002.

Patsy Westcott
Why Do People Take Drugs? Austin: Raintree Steck-Vaughn, 2001.

William L. White
Slaying the Dragon: The History of Addiction Treatment and Recovery in America. Bloomington, IL: Chestnut Health Systems, 1998.

Kimberly S. Young
Caught in the Net: How to Recognize the Signs of Internet Addiction—and a Winning Strategy for Recovery. New York: J. Wiley, 1998.

Kimberly S. Young
Tangled in the Web: Understanding Cybersex from Fantasy to Addiction. Bloomington, IN: 1st Books, 2001.

Index